OCEAN FISHING

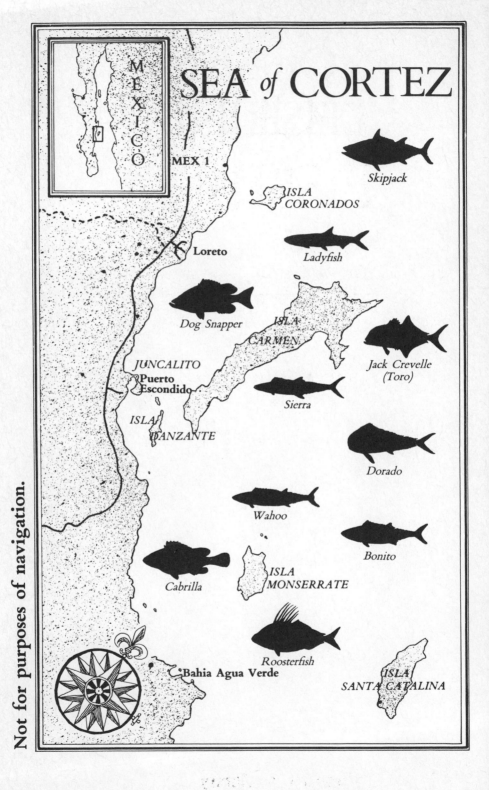

SEA *of* **CORTEZ**

OCEAN FISHING

A Basic Guide for the Saltwater Angler

MICHAEL BAUGHMAN

Illustrated by Frank Lang

PRENTICE HALL PRESS • NEW YORK

Published by Prentice Hall Press
A Division of Simon & Schuster, Inc.
Gulf + Western Building
One Gulf + Western Plaza
New York, NY 10023

PRENTICE HALL PRESS is a trademark of Simon & Schuster, Inc.

Library of Congress Cataloging-in-Publication Data
Baughman, Mike.
Ocean fishing.
Based on author's *Sports Illustrated* articles.
Includes index.
1. Saltwater fishing. I. Title.
SH457.B375 1986   799.1′6   85-30163
ISBN 0-13-629619-X

Manufactured in the United States of America

10 9 8 7 6 5 4 3 2 1

First Edition

To my mother

Acknowledgments

My wife, son, and daughter (Hilde, Pete, and Ingrid) helped greatly in collecting material for this book. For more than twenty years they have been my valued companions on hundreds of fishing trips, and without them much of what is recounted here could not have happened. Most of my fishing writing in recent years has been done for senior editor Linda Verigan of *Sports Illustrated,* and her suggestions and encouragement have been deeply appreciated. Some of the material in the book originally appeared in that magazine. Frank Lang's drawings are art as well as illustration, and I thank him for enlivening the book with them. Finally, I want to express sincere appreciation to Mr. Leon Chandler and the Cortland Line Company for their assistance and cooperation.

Contents

PART THREE • PRACTICAL MATTERS

Preface

I've been fishing in oceans for more than thirty-five years, and the first part of this book consists of personal accounts of some of the most exciting and meaningful of my experiences. Included are chapters on spearfishing, fishing from shore, fishing from a small boat, and, finally, fishing from a large boat for marlin. Each of these pastimes has its own special charms and challenges.

The second part of the book contains specific information about a representative sampling of the hundreds of species of gamefish available to saltwater anglers. There are recommendations regarding techniques, tackle, baits, and lures, and there are also first-person accounts of catching—or trying to catch—each species. These accounts are meant to show *what it is like* to catch the various fish, which is at least as important as knowing *how* to catch them.

Part Three is made up of practical information on a number of matters: rods, reels, lines, knots, lures, baits, and more.

I simply can't imagine a life without ocean fishing, and for as long as I'm able to lift a rod I'll be casting flies, lures, and baits into one sea or another. I wish the same for you.

PART ONE

BASIC EXPERIENCES

The Appeal of the Seas

For the first ten years of my life I lived in a small town near Pittsburgh, Pennsylvania. My happiest memories of those days are of the summer vacations I spent at my great-grandparents' farm near Ligonier, where the principal attraction was a trout stream, which I fished with very moderate success every chance I got. The fish were surely there, though—big brown trout that Grandfather Brant and his pals caught in the dead of night by moonlight. Sometimes when I came down for breakfast early in the morning, two or three large browns lay in state by the kitchen sink. To me they looked like whales, but I imagine they were three- and four-pounders. One thing I know for certain is that those fish and that place affected me as deeply as anything I saw or experienced through my first decade of life, and I've been a fisherman ever since.

Then, when I was eleven, my fishing horizons expanded suddenly and enormously. My father was one of the tens of thousands of Americans who headed west in the years after World War II, looking for jobs, space, and money. He outdid most of his fellow migrants, though, because we ended up in Honolulu, Hawaii.

That entire trip is another clear memory, because I was looking forward to my first glimpse of the Pacific Ocean the whole way. We were two weeks in an old Chevrolet to California and barely arrived in time to catch our plane. The Bay Area was foggy, so I never saw the ocean there.

We took off from San Francisco in the morning, in a DC–6, and it was twelve very long hours to Honolulu. I became sick about the time we reached cruising altitude, and I stayed sick the whole way. To make matters worse, we were either over clouds or in them all the way, and though we crossed more than 2000 miles of the Pacific, I never laid eyes on it once.

When we arrived, it was dark, and warm rain was falling. We took a taxi to our hotel, which turned out to be the Edgewater, very near the beach at Waikiki. That's what my parents told me, at any rate. I fell into bed that night about 5000 miles from my school and friends and the only world I had ever known, and I fell asleep wondering if there really was a Pacific Ocean anyway —and if there was, if ever I'd actually get to see it.

When I woke up early the next morning, sunlight was streaming through the window near my bed. The sky outside, visible through palm fronds, was perfectly clear and deep blue. It probably took me fifteen or twenty seconds to dress, and my parents were still sound asleep when I left the room and closed the door quietly behind me.

Somehow, I instinctively knew the direction to take to get to the beach, which turned out to be no more than 200 yards away. I walked along a narrow concrete pathway through plumeria trees and red and yellow hibiscus plants, the smell of their blossoms powerful in the warm, heavy air. Coconut palms lined the way, their green fronds clattering softly in the offshore wind. I walked over a small rise and through a narrow gap in a concrete beach wall, and there it was. Even at the age of eleven I somehow knew, and was glad, that my life would never be the same again.

This was December, close to Christmas. Back in Pittsburgh, snow covered the ground, and it had been turned from white to gray by soot from the steel mills. Here there was a curve of white sand beach and clear, blue-green water as far as I could see, a mile or more, all the way to Diamond Head, which was silhouetted darkly in the morning light. There were only two hotels on this long stretch of lovely beach—the Royal Hawaiian and the Moana, I would later learn—and no more than a dozen people that I could see. Beyond the blue-green shallows, a quarter mile out, the sea turned deep blue and stayed that way to the horizon. The only waves were those that broke on the beach and rolled up the gentle slope of smooth sand nearly to where I stood, then hissed back out again, leaving a shining film of water in the sunlight.

A Hawaiian boy about my age came down the beach on the wet sand, just a few yards away, and he looked at me and smiled as he passed by. He was wet from swimming, water still running down his brown body. Heading toward Diamond Head, he carried a five-foot metal spear and a pair of goggles in one hand, and a string of fish in the other. There were at least a dozen fish, and they were without doubt the most beautiful and amazing things I'd ever seen: blue, red, green, yellow, and silver, striped and spotted, of various shapes and sizes.

For the next eight years—the entire time I lived in Hawaii—the ocean was the major influence on my life. My parents were kind and affluent enough to buy me a membership in the Outrigger Canoe Club, which in those days was located between the Royal Hawaiian and Moana hotels at the very heart of Waikiki. I took advantage of every activity the club had to offer, which included outrigger canoe races, volleyball, and surfing. At Punahou School, a few miles away in Manoa Valley, I competed in football, basketball, and track. My main love, though, was fishing. I learned how to dive for lobsters. I learned how to spear fish, how to cast for them, and how to troll. I fished off piers and beaches, from canoes, from rowboats and motorboats, and from cabin cruisers. I used everything from handlines to expensive (borrowed) tackle. I loved it all, and I learned most of what I learned the hard, slow way —through trial and error. The errors included encounters with sharks and moray eels, and with dangerous currents and sudden, violent tropical storms.

Since leaving Hawaii in 1955, I've never lived more than three hours from an ocean, except when on a tour of army duty in Germany. Since 1966 I've been with my family in Oregon, where we've learned about salmon, steelhead, and trout, and where we've fished long and hard for them through every season of the year.

The ocean is still the main attraction here, however, and growing more so all the time. There are several reasons for this, the first of them merely practical. Freshwater fishing in Oregon and in all of North America is deteriorating rapidly. Lakes and streams have been dammed, polluted, drained, and fished out, and hatcheries have had to replace native fish populations with their far inferior hatchery products. The trout stream I grew up with, on my great-grandparents' farm, is fishless now and flows through a golf course.

Most of the truly good fishing waters that somehow do survive are either privately controlled (and very expensive) or overcrowded. For that matter, even most mediocre and poor waters are overcrowded, and opening day has become nothing more than a good time to stay home, or perhaps to play golf. Even anglers familiar with Alaskan waters will tell you in no uncertain terms that things are getting worse there all the time, with no relief in sight.

Certainly there is still good freshwater fishing to be had, and I expect to be able to find some and enjoy its fascinations and excitements as long as I live. Yet each year my experiences make it clearer to me that the ocean is the only true wilderness left on earth, and that even though it too suffers from pollution and overfishing, its vastness has done much to protect it from man.

Fresh water covers about 2 percent of the earth's surface, salt water more than 70 percent, a fact that speaks quite plainly for itself. The seas contain 330 million cubic miles of water. Mt. Everest, at 29,028 feet, could be sunk without a trace in the Mariana Trench in the western Pacific. If all the earth's surface irregularities were smoothed out, salt water would cover the entire surface to a depth of about 12,000 feet. It is this enormous volume of water that makes the seas exciting, mysterious, and unpredictable, as well as relatively unexplored and unspoiled.

No one knows what may live in the oceans, and a fisherman never knows what he might hook there. In an *Esquire* magazine article published in the 1930s, Ernest Hemingway wrote of a Cuban fisherman named Carlos who hooked an 80-pound white marlin on a handline in deep water in the Gulf Stream. The fish jumped twice and sounded, and suddenly Carlos felt an enormous weight at the end of the line. A few minutes and hundreds of feet of line later, when the strain finally lessened, he pulled his marlin up. It was dead. A larger marlin, or possibly a swordfish, had bitten across it and crushed it to death. A fish capable of doing that had to weigh several thousand pounds.

I've had my own surprises. Once, when I was a boy in Hawaii, a friend and I were anchored about a mile off Waikiki in a two-man outrigger canoe in about 100 feet of clear water. We were handlining that day, hanging hooks baited with whole prawns over the side. For a couple of hours we caught what we thought we'd catch, which was reef fish of various sizes and species, none of them weighing over a couple of pounds. Just before midday I hauled in a bright silver fish about a foot long—some sort of mackerel, I thought—and decided to use it as bait, just to see what, if anything, would happen. I hooked it carefully through the lip, and a lead sinker took it to the water's bottom. I sat there patiently for more than half an hour, and nothing touched it.

Before we ate lunch I pulled my baitfish up to be sure it was still alive, then tied my line to the outrigger with the silver fish no more than ten or twelve feet down, directly underneath the canoe. A few minutes later, when I was about halfway through my second ham sandwich, I saw a dark shadow passing underneath us. I could tell for sure from the shape that it wasn't a shark, but certainly a fish. What kind of fish it might have been I have no idea. Our canoe was about 12 feet long, and the shadow was even *longer.* I remember staring at it through the clear water, my heart pounding, my mouth open, the sandwich held in front of it.

Whatever it was took my baitfish. The line tied to the outrigger tightened. The canoe slowly turned, then began to move straight out to sea. Within seconds the anchor rope tightened, and the fishing line snapped loudly. I could still see the long shadow a few yards ahead of the canoe now, and it never hesitated or made any movement to indicate that anything unusual had happened. That fish was so large and strong that it apparently hadn't even felt the weight of a 12-foot koa wood canoe with two people in it.

We pulled up anchor and paddled toward shore to shallow water. We spent the rest of the day fishing with our prawns. That was the biggest one that ever got away, and I'm glad it did.

A couple of years ago I took my daughter Ingrid on a fishing vacation to the Sea of Cortez. It was July, very hot and humid, with the sea as flat as glass to the horizon day after day. Dorado, or dolphinfish, were in the Loreto-Mulege area, which was usual for that time of year. There were also huge schools of yellowfin tuna.

The tuna were averaging around twenty pounds, and once a boat got into a school of them it was virtually impossible not to catch any. Schools weren't hard to find, either, because they often fed at the surface, sometimes churning an area half the size of a football field to foam.

One day Ingrid, a boy named Steve she had met at the hotel, and I were trolling white-feathered lures from a fiberglass skiff about three miles offshore, near Carmen Island. Actually, Ingrid and Steve were doing the trolling, and I had a fly rod along, in case we happened upon a casting opportunity for dorado.

By 10:00 A.M. we had already hooked several good fish. Then we came upon a school of tuna that was larger than any we'd seen. There must have been several thousand fish in it, and as soon as we reached the edge of the school both Ingrid and Steve had hookups.

I relaxed and watched them fight their fish for a few minutes, and then I watched the school of tuna move slowly off, feeding their way toward Carmen. Little silver mackerel broke the surface by the hundreds in their panic as the tuna attacked them. We could find tuna again, I was sure.

When Ingrid and Steve both had their fish well under control, and I was sure I wouldn't get in their way, I decided to make a few casts with the fly rod, just for something to do. Tied to the 12-pound test leader tippet was a rather small orange-and-white maribou muddler fly, a pattern that I used in Oregon for summer steelhead and that had also worked for dorado up to ten pounds.

I certainly didn't expect to catch anything. The odds against casting blindly and hooking a dorado were no better than a thousand to one. The most I could reasonably hope for—a possibility somewhat less remote—was a bonito of 3 or 4 pounds.

So I lazily worked out line until I was false-casting 50 feet, then dropped the fly onto the smooth surface. It didn't sink, so I jerked hard at the line to try to drag it under. The surface exploded. A great boil appeared on the water where the fly had been—much like the boil a large trout makes when it inhales a dry fly—and then something huge was thrashing wildly out there, throwing silver spray in all directions. Then it took off.

I was using excellent tackle—a stiff 9½ foot rod and a saltwater reel with 250 yards of nylon backing behind the fly line. Everything was gone in about fifteen seconds. Though I palmed the reel hard to increase the pressure, the run of that fish grew stronger and faster all the time, until it hit the end of the line and snapped the leader at the fly.

I still lie in bed at night wondering what that fish was. What could do that? On that same tackle I had landed tuna rather easily, as well as roosterfish weighing up to 40 pounds. Whatever hit the little muddler felt ten or fifteen times as strong and twice as fast as either of those fish.

Blue marlin are said to swim at speeds of up to 50 miles per hour, and dorado can approach 40 miles per hour. Perhaps the fish that cleaned me out was a large dorado, but I'll never know for sure, and nothing quite like that is ever likely to happen to me again. But something else will—something equally exciting and unexpected.

Diversity, unpredictability, surprise—along with the beauty of the seas and the creatures in and around them—are the strong appeals of ocean fishing. During my years in Hawaii I probably went spearfishing between four and five hundred times. I can honestly say that on each of those trips I saw or experienced at least one thing that I'd never seen or experienced before.

It was inevitable, because more than 20,000 species of fish live in salt water, with countless varieties of other swimming, crawling, and stationary creatures. Sea life ranges in size from microscopic diatoms to blue whales of more than one hundred tons. The fish themselves range from barely visible gobies to billfish and sharks more than 20 feet long.

Though it may seem savage to some human sensibilities, nearly every fish in the ocean sooner or later becomes a meal. The sea is one huge food chain. At any given time, an average crustacean will have more than 100,000 diatoms in its stomach. An average herring will have as many as 5000 crustaceans in its stomach and a humpback whale requires a ton of herring to temporarily satisfy its appetite. Such is life, and death, in the ocean.

Many years ago when I was fishing off Marathon Key in Florida, I clearly saw this food chain in action. No more than 30 feet from my boat a large school of 6-inch baitfish broke the surface together—hundreds of them, shining silver in the sunlight as they sailed six feet or more through the air in a mass—and then entered the water again and streaked off to sea just inches beneath the surface. Just behind the bait fish, chasing them, was a school of what looked like fifteen or twenty small bonito. A few feet behind the bonito, and chasing them, was a group of half a dozen large jacks. Just behind the jacks, and closing distance fast, was one very large fish that I couldn't identify. Most likely, each predator I saw caught some of the others.

An ocean fisherman with his baits, lures, and flies becomes a temporary and artificial part of this food chain. In a more direct way, so does a spearfisherman. There are really only four ways to fish in the sea: still fishing, trolling, casting, and spearing. There are also only four ways in which this fishing can be accomplished: from shore, from a small boat, from a large boat, or in the water with a spear. Nevertheless, there is far too much to know about ocean fishing for any reasonable person to consider himself a bona fide expert, except perhaps in regard to the two or three places or species of fish he knows best.

But I've tried nearly every kind of fishing the oceans have to offer, in many places, and I've learned that each place and each fish is different in many ways from all the others. Yet there are certain similarities too, certain basics that are worth knowing wherever you are.

My own preferences in fishing techniques, as I'll make clear, always tend toward what I would call effective simplicity. The technological age, even the computer age, has caught up with fishing, and particularly with ocean fishing. Though this sophistication may result in more fish hooked and landed, I'm by no means convinced that it gives us more pleasure.

This, then, brings us back to diversity, unpredictability, surprise, and the raw excitement they generate. I believe that these elements contribute much to the attraction of ocean fishing. I also believe that an approach to fishing that emphasizes pleasure well above technological gadgetry is best. Most of what I have to say in this book relates in one way or another to these beliefs.

Spearing and Diving

Ambrose Bierce included the following definition in his *Devil's Dictionary:* "Ocean: a body of water occupying about two thirds of a world made for man—who has no gills."

Bierce had a sharp sense of humor, but as far as man's relationship to water is concerned, he didn't do his research. The truth is, several thousand generations ago the human foot was a fin, and we did indeed have gills. I doubt it's a coincidence that about 70 percent of the earth's surface is covered with water and that about 70 percent of the human body is also composed of water. It's reasonable to conclude that there is a natural bond at work here which accounts for a good part of the strong appeal that water holds for fishermen.

This brings me to spearfishing, the most elemental way a human being can pursue and capture a fish. We can't fly after birds, and few of us can run after and capture game animals, but any healthy swimmer can, for a few dollars, get equipped to enter the sea and become a part of a fascinating new world.

Spearing was the first kind of ocean fishing I learned. The moment I saw the Hawaiian boy with his string of brightly colored fish, I knew I had to learn to spear. Until then the only swimming I'd ever done was in a neighborhood pool near Pittsburgh and at a two-week summer camp on Lake Erie, but within a month after we moved to Honolulu I had a spear and sling, a diving mask, and swim fins, and was exploring the shallow waters off Waikiki. Soon I became familiar with Portlock, Makapuu, Sand Beach, and Laie. I learned the names of the fish, and became familiar with different kinds of seaweed and coral, with deep ledges and sunken boats. The hundreds of hours I spent spearfishing taught me a great deal about oceans and their life. I can even say that spearing had more to do with my growing up—as opposed to merely growing older—than any other single factor through my junior high and high school years. A couple of my most memorable experiences—involving a moray eel and a shark—will show what I mean.

When I was thirteen years old, there was a group of seven or eight of us who hung out together at the Outrigger Club. We were just breaking into sports at Punahou School, starting to drink a little Primo beer, and trying hard to convince ourselves and anybody else who would pay any attention that we were kids no longer, but young men to be taken seriously.

In the beach's caste system, the single group that we wanted most to impress was the beachboys. These weren't college drop-outs, or gigolos, or hustlers after an easy few dollars. Generally they were big, tough, quiet men—mostly Hawaiians or Samoans—who worked on the beach because they loved it there. Chick, Steamboat, Rabbit, Blue, Panama, and a dozen others were so widely known and respected that a casual smile or brief nod from one of them could make my day.

One summer morning I finally had a chance to prove how much of a man I had become. I had arrived at the club early, about 8:00 A.M., which was long before I could expect to see my friends. As soon as I'd changed into my swimming shorts I walked through the passageway from the clubhouse out between the canoe sheds to the deserted beach. The sea was unusually calm, the tide low, the water very clear. Conditions were ideal for spearing fish.

I was thinking of going out alone when Sammy came along the passageway behind me. Sammy was a beachboy, a powerfully built Hawaiian of thirty or so, easygoing and willing to laugh at nearly anything until he had had a few drinks. Then he quickly became a person well worth steering clear of. I had watched him in a fight once, down near the Waikiki Tavern—a short and very impressive fight.

When I heard him coming and turned, he smiled at me, apparently happy with the morning and with his life in general as well. "Good day to spear," he said. "See that? Low and clear. Want to go?"

"With you?"

"Who else? Nobody else around here, bruddah."

"Sure, I'll go."

"You got stuff?"

"Sure, in my locker."

"Go get it. I'll see you by the canoe."

Five minutes later we had loaded in the spears, slings, fins, masks, a bailing bucket, and an anchor. Paddling out—I was in front, Sammy was steering—we moved quickly along, the bow of the canoe lifting and dropping over the small swells that built near shore. I was a decent paddler and in good shape, and I pulled hard with a quick stroke to prove what I could do.

"Take it easy, bruddah," Sammy told me. "We got a long way to go. Can you dive thirty feet?"

I was used to spearing in depths of from 6 to 12 feet. "Sure," I said. "I

12

can do it." If he'd asked me if I could dive 100 feet, I'd have given the same answer.

We did go a long way out, far beyond the reefs I was familiar with. The water was deep, clear, blue.

"Drop it," Sammy finally said.

I lifted the anchor overboard, let it go, and watched the rope play out and down. When it finally stopped, we drifted for a few more seconds with the gentle offshore wind. Then somewhere down there the anchor caught, jolting us, turning the bow toward shore. We were out so far that the pink Royal Hawaiian Hotel and white Moana looked small, and the club between them could barely be seen. The beach itself was a thin white line, glaring in the sunlight.

"The ledge we want is close by here," Sammy said, "Plenty *kumu,* maybe an *uhu* too." Smiling widely, he worked the swim fins on. Then he spit into the mask and rubbed the saliva over the glass to keep it from fogging with body heat, washed it out, and pulled it on. He grabbed his spear and sling. "Follow me, bruddah," he said. He swung his legs over the gunwale, then dropped feet first into the sea.

I followed Sammy. About 50 yards from the canoe he found the ledge, which was cut so deeply into the floor of the reef that it might have been called a cave. The opening was at least 20 feet across, 3 or 4 feet high, and across the length of it fish of all kinds could be seen swimming slowly in and out of shadow. It was an ideal spot, because there was no other cover nearby. Except for a few small coral clumps, the bottom was flat and gray around the ledge as far as I could see.

But the fish were so far down that it was hard to distinguish their colors. Distances underwater are deceptive, but it looked like more than 30 feet to me. It looked like fifty. I had doubts about reaching the bottom, but I knew I'd have to try, because in my mind failure would mean humiliation.

First I watched Sammy dive, and he made it look easy. Kicking smoothly, pulling hard with his free right arm, spear and sling held out ahead in his left hand, he glided quickly downward. About halfway to the bottom he held his mask against his face and blew, relieving the ear pressure. Then he kicked to the bottom, leveled off, held to the roof of the ledge with one hand, and peered into the opening. He was at the middle of the ledge. He looked both ways, and after a few seconds swam to his left, quickly drew his spear back in the sling, aimed, and let it go. Whatever he had aimed at he had hit. Two feet of the 6-foot spear protruded from the ledge, vibrating from the struggles of the fish. Sammy grabbed the spear, but he didn't come up. Instead, he fitted

13

the notched end back in the sling, and then slowly worked from left to right across the ledge. Twice more he shot, the last time near the right-hand edge, and after that he finally surfaced. Three fish were impaled on his spear, two red *kumus* and a small blue *uhu*. I guessed that he had been down at least two minutes. When he broke the surface near me he smiled from behind the mask, dark hair matted wet against his forehead. "Your turn, bruddah," he said.

"You can go again," I said. "If you want I'll take those back to the canoe."

"I can do that. First I watch you."

With the sun warm on my shoulders and back, and the ledge looking farther down than ever, I took deep breaths to clear and expand my lungs. I dove, trying to relax, trying to imitate Sammy, kicking and pulling smoothly, slowly, and with controlled power, conserving oxygen. About halfway down I popped my ears. The pressure was partly relieved, but the last few feet down to the ledge there was steadily increasing pain. Near the bottom the water was very cool. I grabbed the roof of the ledge with my left hand, the rock rough and cold to the touch, and, head pounding, ears aching, lungs already straining toward another breath, I looked back into the shadow. And shadow was all I saw. The fish had scattered to the side of the ledge or further into it. I released my grip, and because Sammy was watching I drew the spear back in the sling and shot it uselessly into the darkness. It hit a fish. Before it had gone three feet the spear thudded into something, and I quickly grabbed the end of the spear and held it tightly, kicking hard toward the flat, silver surface far above. When I broke the surface I gasped for breath. I barely heard Sammy beside me.

"What you want a *palani* for?"

Still panting—and trying not to—I looked at my fish. It was a 4-pound *palani,* a flat brown trash fish. No one ever bothered with *palani.* "Couldn't tell what it was," I managed between breaths. "Looked like an *uhu* to me."

"Yeah?" Sammy said. "Sure. That can happen. Let's get these back to the canoe."

Before we swam to the canoe I emptied out my mask. There was a fair amount of blood in it. Something in my nose had ruptured from the pressure. I felt vaguely sick to my stomach. Perhaps I had been underwater for a minute, certainly no longer than that, and it had nearly ruined me. It was wild luck that I had hit even a *palani,* and soon I would have to dive again.

We dumped the fish into the canoe, then held onto the gunwale for rest.

"You see that moray?" Sammy asked me.

"Moray? No."

"It's there. Big one. I saw him right when I speared the *uhu.*"

14

"How big?"

"Maybe four feet. Maybe five. Big."

"I didn't see it."

"He's way back. You ready to spear 'im, bruddah?"

"Sure," I said.

I followed Sammy back to the ledge. It was only 50 yards away, but I had time to remember every moray I'd ever seen, and all that I'd heard or read about them. They were evil-looking creatures, nothing to them but powerful muscle and needle-sharp teeth. When you saw a moray come out of a hole in a reef, with its wicked little eyes and its mouth opening and closing with every respiration, it was time to move along. Morays are known to defend their territories. Once when two of us were gathering lobsters along a shallow reef across the island, a small moray struck like a snake, its head crashing into my friend's mask, shattering the thick glass and causing fragments to slash his nose and both cheeks open. There were also rare instances of morays attacking for no apparent reason. I had read of a huge moray coming up through and all the way out of 30 feet of water, to strike at a diver's head. The diver, swimming on his back at the time, protected himself with his arm, which was almost severed by a single bite. He nearly bled to death before he was rescued and taken back to shore. Once I had worked up the courage to spear a large moray myself. I hit it in the neck, and it wrapped itself around the spear and attacked it, teeth grinding loudly against the metal. By the time it died, the spear had been twisted out of shape by the writhing body.

So I wanted nothing to do with spearing a 5-foot moray, though nothing could have made me admit that to anyone but myself.

We were over the ledge. I could see fish again, many of them, drifting in and out of shadow. The sun was hot on my shoulders and back. "I'll dive first," Sammy said. "I'll get him in the head. If he takes off from the ledge across the bottom, you dive. Try to get him again. If he stays in there, you wait till I come up. Okay? You got that?"

"Sure," I said. "But what if he goes after you?"

"Then, bruddah, you'll see a Hawaiian swim like hell. Okay. Here goes."

Sammy dove. Why did he do it? Was he showing off? It wasn't likely that he'd bother showing off for me. He probably wanted the moray out of his favorite ledge. That made sense. I was praying he'd kill it, terrified at the prospect of having to dive again myself.

He flattened out against the bottom, this time at the left-hand edge of the ledge. Slowly, using his left hand to pull himself along, he worked his way across. Just past the middle of the ledge he slipped in under the roof until he

15

disappeared to his knees. Already he had been down for more than a minute. Then he moved farther in. All I could see were the tips of his bright green swim fins, motionless, far below me. When the fins completely disappeared he had been down about a minute and a half.

Another full minute after that he came out head first, kicking hard for the surface, with no spear and his right arm trailing blood in the water, a pinkish trail that quickly spread and disappeared.

When he broke the surface next to me he barely paused for breath. "Gimme your spear, bruddah!"

I gave it to him gladly, and he fitted it into his own sling.

"What about your arm?" I asked.

"Only a coral cut."

He dove again then, reaching the bottom more quickly this time, kicking straight in under the roof of the ledge at the place he had come out before. About two minutes later he came out again, slowly now, dragging a spear. Then the moray appeared. It was huge, with both spears through its head. It was dead. Sammy dragged it up behind him to the surface.

"That's enough for me," he said. "*You* want to spear some more? You want to stay?"

"No thanks," I said. I was staring at the moray. I'd never seen one nearly so large. It was at least 5 feet long.

"I can sell this to a pro wrestler staying at the Royal," Sammy said as we swam back to the canoe. "He told me he wanted an eel. He's from someplace like Germany or something. I guess they eat all kinds of things there."

We paddled toward shore. "Short trip," Sammy said. "Bleeding stopped. Tough moray. Wore me out in there. I sell it, you keep the fish. Okay?"

"You sure? Okay. Thanks."

"You like spearing way out here?"

"Sure. I kind of wish I'd had a try at the moray, though."

"Yeah? Maybe next time."

"Maybe," I said.

I never asked Sammy exactly what had gone on there underneath the ledge. Somehow, I really didn't want to know about it.

All the way back in I thanked God I hadn't had to try.

Because the experience with Sammy made me painfully aware of my limitations, I began to take diving and spearing more seriously than ever. I think most of us react that way when we spend a day with someone who's really good at a type of fishing we only think we're good at. In any case, I began to spear—on the best days, from seven in the morning until dinnertime without a break. I learned of places with spiny lobsters and rock lobsters that no one else knew about. I discovered dozens of reefs and ledges full of *kumu, aholehole,* and *aveveo.* I even bought a surplus World War II navy frogman's aqualung at Pearl Harbor. The tank held only fifteen minutes' worth of air and was surely primitive by today's standards, but it worked, and the first few times I dove I found it splendid. But its novelty soon wore off, and when it did I went back to the simplicity of free diving. Occasionally I still dive with scuba gear, but, as my mother-in-law in Germany often says, "The more you have, the more you have to worry about." Diving with a mask, a spear, and a simple Hawaiian sling certainly imposes limitations, but it is also easy, inexpensive, and, to me, more rewarding.

So I did become a good diver and spearfisherman, and by the time I was seventeen years old I was sure I was ready for anything the Pacific Ocean had to offer. Then came the summer of the shark.

That year I began to spear with a close friend named Robert. Though Robert and I got along very well, we were different in nearly every way. Our personalities and our physical abilities clashed. We never talked about the matter or even acknowledged it, but we were always competing, trying to do whatever we did as well as we could in attempts to temporarily overshadow each other. Among athletic high school boys who are sure they have become young men, such competition is normal enough, but our rivalry was somewhat unique in that there was no way we *could* legitimately match ourselves against each other.

I couldn't give Robert a contest in anything involving strength or speed. He could do as many push-ups with one hand as I could do with two. He was Punahou School's fastest sprinter, and he was a good running back too—when he didn't fumble the handoff or pitchout. His athletic shortcoming was a lack of coordination; throwing or catching a ball was exceedingly difficult for him. When we played doubles volleyball on the sand courts at the Outrigger Club during summer vacations, it was as if his hands had been dipped in cement.

Good coordination and bigger-than-average hands were the only real athletic gifts I had. Though not exceptionally fast, and not unusually big either, I could generally catch a forward pass if I could touch it, and basketball and volleyball came easily for me.

The real reason Robert and I spent so much time spearing together that year was that we had discovered it was one activity in which we could compete on equal terms. For a period of more than a month we spent nearly every day at the beach, and if the waves were down and the water was clear (and if there weren't any exceptionally lovely tourist girls down at the beach in front of the Royal Hawaiian Hotel) we would check out a two-man canoe from Sally Hale at the Outrigger Club beach shack and paddle out to the old barge to spear some fish.

The sunken barge was about a half mile out, past Baby Surf and then a little west toward Pearl Harbor. It was widely believed that the barge had gone down during the Japanese attack on Pearl Harbor, and no one I knew ever questioned the story. To spear fish at the site of one of the most significant events in American history gave us a sense of eerie adventure.

Our spearfishing was a ritual. We would start out fairly early in the morning, warming as we paddled, with the bow of the canoe slapping down against the water as we slid over the Baby Surf swells. Beyond Baby Surf the white sand bottom was furrowed by the current and marked with small outcroppings of coral. Just short of the barge were coral walls and ledges at depths of 10 to 12 feet. When we dropped anchor there it caught on the bottom within seconds, the rope tightening, then creaking, as the canoe moved seaward in the breeze.

We pulled on our masks, then slipped into one swim fin apiece, the idea being that fatigue and leg cramps could be avoided by changing the fin from one foot to the other every hour or so. Spears fitted into our slings, we dropped over the side into the pleasant shock of cool, clear water.

Some days we stayed out at the barge for as long as six or eight hours, spearing the entire time, and returning to the canoe only to dump more fish into it. Robert kept his fish in the bow and I kept mine in the stern, with the sections divided by the bailing bucket. There were two divisions of competition that we recognized. One was the number of fish we each caught, and the other was the number of "good" fish we speared. The common fish—*palani, manini,* and *hinalea*—were abundant, and anyone who could dive to the bottom and aim a spear could get about as many of them as he wanted. The desired reef fish in Hawaii—those considered the best for eating—were *kumu, aveoveo,* and *aholehole.* These fish were always much more difficult to find, for they normally stayed out of sight, far back in holes and ledges.

I was more accurate with a spear than Robert, but he was a stronger swimmer and diver and had more breath, so we usually broke even. I would end up with the most fish, but he would get more of the good ones. He was especially effective when it came to exploring the deep recesses of the old barge. In the twisted remains, with the metal grown over with coral and seaweed, there were places where Robert would swim until he was completely

18

out of sight, just as Sammy had done at the ledge with the moray. Then, after fifteen or twenty seconds, Robert would emerge, either with a good fish on his spear or swearing underwater at his miss, the bubbles rising to the surface just ahead of him.

The real winner in our spearing competition was Chick Daniels, the Hawaiian beachboy at the Royal. We gave him all our fish in return for telling us of any recently arrived, good-looking tourist girls at the hotel.

It was the shark that finally ended our competition. I think it was a blue shark, identified by its color, slender shape, and extremely long pectoral fins.

It was on our third or fourth trip out to the barge that the shark appeared for the first time. Both Robert and I had just dumped some fish into the canoe and were swimming back toward the barge together when it showed about 50 feet away, perhaps 3 feet beneath the surface on the seaward side of the barge, swimming very slowly—but straight toward us. It appeared that the shark saw us just when we saw it, because as we stopped in the water, it turned at a slight angle and stayed there motionless, apparently staring back at us.

All of this happened in less than a second. Within that second, both Robert and I panicked, then caught ourselves and pretended that we hadn't.

I can't guess what the shark may have felt, if anything, but after hanging there for a few seconds it turned away, and with one easy pump of its slender tail swam slowly straight out to sea.

Robert and I watched it go, and after it was out of sight and we were positive it wasn't circling back, we swam to the barge to spear more fish, acting as if nothing special had happened.

It was that afternoon that our bragging began. After we had convinced ourselves that it wasn't an awfully large shark, and that sharks were really nothing to be frightened of anyway, our conversation went like this:

"All you have to do is be careful when you aim," I explained. "If you get the spear in right behind the eye, you've got the son-of-a-bitch."

"If he came right at me, I'd put it right between his eyes."

"I wouldn't. I'd just slip off to the side at the last second and put it behind the eye. It's supposed to be the best place. You know that."

"What the hell," Robert said. "You trying to tell me between the eyes wouldn't work?"

"Maybe there's more cartilage there for the spear to go through that way. Maybe the spear would bounce off."

"Bounce off, hell. My sling's strong enough, and I am too."

"What would you do if you missed?"

19

"Scream underwater at it. They can't stand that sound. You know that."

"It's *supposed* to scare them. Who do we know who's ever tried it, though?"

"Who's going to miss? Hell, John Hanl speared a seven-foot shark out behind Queen's Surf last year."

"I'll try, if I ever get a chance," I said.

"Not if I get a chance first you won't."

There was a lot of talk like that, and we saw the shark nearly every day. We theorized that the sunken barge was a regular stop on its feeding circuit. Each time we saw it, the shark would appear near the limit of our underwater vision, fifty or sixty feet away and a few feet beneath the surface. Prisms of light reflected off its smooth, bluish back. And each time it saw us, or sensed our presence, it would stop, hold there for a while, then turn and swim slowly away.

Later, paddling in, we would talk about the possibility of chasing it, or luring it toward us.

"We could always try swimming after it," Robert said, "but if it's scared of us, there's no way we could ever catch up."

"Hell no. We could try luring it in with some dead, bloody fish, but it doesn't look starved or anything. I guess we'll have to wait and see if it comes to us."

"Damn right. No problem there."

And it finally did come to us, on a late afternoon near the end of August. Robert had just speared a good *kumu* in a deep ledge close to the barge, and he had brought it up to the surface and was swimming toward me to show it off. Once again, we saw the shark at the same moment. As usual, it stopped some 50 feet away, turned at a slight angle to us, then held there, motionless, blue-backed and white-bellied, just beneath the surface.

Robert and I were no more than 10 feet apart at the time, and we stayed where we were, expecting that after a few seconds the shark would turn away from us and swim out to sea, as it always had before.

But this time the seconds dragged on and became half a minute or more, and then it started straight at us, slowly, but without hesitation. The next thing I knew I was swimming. Without being conscious of it, I had dropped my spear and sling and turned, and, in a sick-stomached, dizzying panic, heart pounding hard in my ears, I churned through the water, straining to reach the canoe.

Robert and I reached it together—the side away from the outrigger was facing us—and we nearly turned it over as we clambered in. If not for the

20

tension of the anchor rope on the other side, I think we would surely have capsized the canoe, and if we had we'd have tried our hardest to swim at that same furious pace the entire half mile to shore.

We sat facing each other in the canoe, six feet apart but reluctant to meet each other's eyes. I took my diving mask off and looked for the shark, but there was no sign of it. When I finally glanced at Robert I noticed that he too had dropped his spear and sling out there somewhere. He was gasping for breath, and trembling. So was I, and we were both pale even through our dark suntans.

We never talked about it, then or later. It didn't matter whether the shark was really coming after us, or if it had been attracted by the fish on Robert's spear. Possibly its swimming in our direction had been nothing more than a coincidence.

But none of that was of any real concern. What did matter was that the way we had revealed ourselves—to ourselves and to each other—turned out to be a good thing. No one grows up through a single experience, but some experiences help a great deal more than others. I don't believe Robert and I ever lied or bragged to each other again about anything. Our inclination to compete with one another also disappeared that afternoon.

After a few minutes' rest we hauled up the anchor and paddled hard for shore, glad to have something to do and to leave the barge behind us. The shark was surely gone by then, but we didn't look for our spears and slings. Halfway in we began to talk of various matters unrelated to what had just happened —the major league baseball season, the trans-Pacific yacht race, whether or not we would get away with buying beer that night at Charlie's Tavern.

Although some of my attitudes about diving have changed considerably over the years, my love for the pastime has remained constant. If anything, I enjoy it more now than I did as a boy in Hawaii. I rarely use a spear anymore, and when I do I still prefer the simplest model I can find—five or six feet long with a hinged barb—with a homemade Hawaiian sling of surgical rubber to go with it. Even today, such an outfit costs only a few dollars. I still don't use a snorkel, though most divers prefer them.

Whenever I travel to salt water I take a diving mask with me, if not a spear. When exploring shallow waters, wearing an old pair of running or tennis shoes is preferable to fins, because they afford protection against coral, urchins, and the very occasional ray or scorpion fish. In deep water, fins are always better, and I still prefer to use only one and occasionally change it from foot to foot when I'm out for longer than a couple of hours.

One hot afternoon in March of 1984 I was very glad I had a diving mask with me. My wife and son and I were trolling at a slow speed from a small boat between Coronado and Carmen islands on the Sea of Cortez. We had seen at least two dozen whales on the surface throughout the day, both blues and finbacks, from a distance of 100 yards and more. Suddenly, about thirty yards directly ahead of the boat, a finback surfaced. I cut the motor at once, and we reeled in our lines, drifting toward the whale.

At least 50 feet long, it spouted shortly after breaking the surface, throwing white spray 15 feet into the air with a loud, whistling exhalation. It lay sideways to us in the water, its dark back shining wetly in the sunlight, with the dorsal fin that gives the species its name clearly visible and its flat head exposed all the way to the eye.

The finback stayed on the surface a minute or two, and we—in our boat that was less than a third of its length—sat there staring at it no more than 30 feet away. The whale must have been aware of our presence, but it showed no sign. Finally, I remembered my diving mask, pulled it on, and dropped over the side to swim up closer to the whale.

Only when I saw the whole whale did I appreciate how huge it really was. Moving slowly toward it through the warm, clear water, I was trying to look at it all at once, and at the same time concentrate on each detail—the slightly opened mouth, the throat furrows, the way the gray back lightened to become a smooth white underside—so as never to forget it.

When I was about 15 feet away, the finback sounded. It raised its head slightly, arched its back and lowered its head, then pumped its great flukes once at the surface, propelling itself downward at an angle of about 45 degrees. As it started down, the surface disturbance that it created hit me. The wave of rushing, bubbling water that washed by and over me was a tangible contact with the whale's animal grace and immense power.

Diving through the clear water, the whale became smaller and smaller, and within seconds after it had started down it disappeared into the darkness of the sea—but when I swam back to the boat I could still feel its exhilarating presence through my skin.

Just a couple of days later I had another valuable diving experience, but this time involving a fish only about 5 inches long.

Each evening for about a week, I had been fly-fishing from Nopolo Point, a few miles south of Loreto. Catches had been fair—good enough to keep me going back—but not spectacular. A couple of hours of casting a red-and-white streamer fly usually produced four or five good fish—sierra, ladyfish, and bonito—up to about 8 pounds each. But I thought I ought to be doing better, because hundreds of fish were actively feeding on schools of bait within easy reach of my casts. The red-and-white fly had worked well on previous trips, but for some reason it wasn't attracting many strikes now.

Finally, I walked down to Nopolo in mid-afternoon to get a closer look at the baitfish schools with my diving mask. To my surprise, I saw that the silver bait fish had yellow stripes across their middles. Back at the hotel I spent the rest of that afternoon tying streamer flies which included strands of yellow bucktail between the white wings and silver bodies. That evening, I caught five times as many fish as I had on any other day.

Scuba (Self-Contained Underwater Breathing Apparatus) gear is widely used today, in all the seas of the earth—even, thanks to wet suits, in the cold ones. Though scuba gear varies considerably in design and price, all outfits work in the same way. There are one or two tanks holding compressed air, and a regulator which automatically feeds a diver air that has the same pressure as the surrounding water. The diver's exhalations escape through an exhaust valve. It is actually a very simple system, yet you certainly need instruction before you attempt using it on your own. A course on the proper use and care of equipment, diving techniques, and safety measures is an absolute must. Because diving is a very popular sport these days, such classes are available in virtually any town within a few hours' drive of an ocean. Equipment is usually provided, which is a good thing, because it would be a mistake for you to invest in scuba gear before you're positive you'll use and enjoy it.

Free diving can be learned without instruction, but you should certainly be a fairly strong swimmer before you try it. If you progress to the point where you are diving in 12 feet of water, there are some discomforts that will likely occur. When you dive down, your mask will have less pressure within it than the water pressure surrounding it, which can cause pain behind your eyes. When this happens, you must exhale through your nose to equalize the pressure in your mask on the way down. Ear pain is another common problem, caused by increased pressure on the outer ear as you dive. When this happens, press the mask against your face and blow, to "pop" your ears and equalize the pressure—or if using goggles, hold your nose and blow.

Unfortunately, too many people stay away from spearfishing and diving because of a fear of sharks. Sensational books and movies show us huge, malevolent creatures whose desire for human blood is unmatched except perhaps by Dracula. There are surely many sharks in the oceans, and they do deserve respect, but the danger of your ever actually being threatened or attacked by one is very remote. To reduce these odds to the edge of impossibility, here are some guidelines:

1. Avoid areas where potentially dangerous sharks have been sighted, or where attacks have occurred in the past.
2. Don't dive in murky water. It isn't much fun anyway, and sharks have poor eyesight, so in murky water they are much more apt to mistake a human for a seal or large fish—creatures they are accustomed to feeding on.
3. Don't ever dive alone.
4. Don't dive with a bleeding wound.
5. If you see a shark, it's best to swim away slowly and calmly—not in a panic, as Robert and I did in Hawaii. Experts believe that thrashing through the water only serves to attract the shark's attention and perhaps even excite it.
6. If a shark approaches you, hit it on the nose with a spear or whatever else may be available. Usually this drives them off.
7. Some people continue to believe that screaming underwater repels sharks. It's true that they are sensitive to sound and vibration, so this *may* be true.
8. A recent study concluded that sharks won't approach divers in black-and-white-striped wetsuits. If this is true, such suits should soon be on the market.
9. Don't tow speared fish near you. It's best to put them in a boat as soon as possible, or, if you spear without a boat, to keep them on a float which you attach to yourself with a cord of at least 30 feet in length.

In all the time I've spent underwater—in Hawaii, the Mediterranean, the South Atlantic, and the Sea of Cortez—I've seen a total of five sharks. The only one that gave any indication it saw me was the shark that Robert and I encountered, and I sincerely doubt that it meant us any harm.

My own feeling is that morays pose a somewhat greater threat to divers than sharks. They are easy to avoid because only rarely do they emerge from their holes and ledges. A diver reaching into these holes and ledges for lobsters can easily provoke a bite from a territorial moray, and even if the bite is on the hand, the heavy glove that should be worn while gathering lobsters offers little protection. If you are diving in an area where morays are known to be numerous, it is probably best to *spear* lobsters. Anytime you stick a hand or foot, or—worse yet—your head, into a dark, protected area underwater, you are running the risk of a moray attack.

Jellyfish are fairly common in all warm seas, and though they are seldom a threat to life, they can inflict severe pain. Once, in Hawaii, I was spearfishing a couple of hundred yards off Makapuu Beach on Oahu. I came up off the bottom in fairly deep water with a good fish on my spear—straight up into a school of Portuguese men-of-war. These are floating jellyfish with long tentacles which wrap around any living thing they touch (in this case, me) and impart a sudden, painful sting.

I swam to shore as quickly as I could and removed the tentacles from my upper body by rubbing the skin hard with sand. I was sick almost to the point of nausea for about half an hour, but then felt good enough to dive again—but in another area.

Usually men-of-war are found in deep water, but if there is an onshore wind they can drift toward beaches. Their floating, gas-filled bodies are easily seen in calm water. In case of a sting, after removing the tentacles with sand, a towel, or a heavy glove, rub the affected area with ammonia or alcohol, or even a small dab of gasoline if nothing else is available.

Most divers who get into trouble have themselves to blame. A prudent person exercising common sense in regard to waves, tides, currents, and weather, who tries to do no more than he or she is capable of doing, and who treats unfamiliar areas with respect, can have a trouble–free lifetime of exciting and enjoyable ocean swimming and diving.

Ambrose Bierce was wrong. It remains human nature to enter the water and to enjoy it for a while.

Fishing from Shore

It was because of spearing that I began to fish seriously with a rod and reel from Hawaiian beaches. One summer day my friend Robert and I drove out around Diamond Head to do some spearing in the deep water off Makapuu, but before we got there we passed a lovely stretch of white sand beach where large waves usually crashed close to shore. That day, though, the sea was calm, and we could tell from the car that the water was clear enough for diving. We decided to try it there while we had the chance.

I don't remember that we speared a single fish off that beach, but it didn't matter, because something more important happened. To our great surprise, we learned that large fish can be found close to shore in fairly shallow water. We saw dozens of big jacks *(ulua)* swimming by, singly and in pairs. There was no cover for them—no rocks or reefs or ledges—so though we chased fish after fish, we never got within even 30 feet of one.

Later that afternoon, back at Waikiki and inspired by what we'd seen, we went spearing in the shallow water directly in front of the Moana Hotel. We had paddled over this area dozens if not hundreds of times without ever considering the possibility that fish could be found there. Again, we were very surprised. No more then 50 yards from where hotel guests ate meals and sipped cocktails on the outdoor banyan patio, in water that at low tide was barely waist-deep, among the rocks and coral formations, we saw and speared at least as many fish as we usually got in water 20 feet deep a half mile offshore.

Ever since that day, rod and reel fishing from shore has been one of my favorite pastimes. Fishing with live and dead bait, Robert and I caught *ulua* from the sandy beach and from other beaches on Oahu, such as Laie and Portlock. We caught bonefish too, without ever realizing that 5000 miles away, in the South Atlantic, they are among the most prized of fish. We caught several species of reef fish, including some of the same ones we had been spearing for years. Fishing with rod and reel also had one obvious advantage over spearing. Whenever we wanted to, we could release our catch unharmed.

Since leaving Hawaii, I've fished from many beaches on many oceans. It is a relatively simple kind of fishing, and can be enjoyed on salt water nearly any place or time of year. *Surf fishing* is the term commonly applied to fishing from land's end, and there are said to be about 5 million surf casters in America. Some of them bundle up in chest waders and rain gear over seven layers of clothing and stand waist deep in roaring waves to cast lures that weigh a quarter pound or more 100 yards out with stiff, 14-foot, two-handed rods. Others hook 20-pound fish with fly rods on casts of 20 feet in water less than 1 foot deep.

I learned about fishing in extremely shallow water in Mexico. In the pale orange light of dawn on the first morning of a ten-day vacation in Loreto, my daughter Ingrid and I were jogging south along a smooth curve of beach not far from Escondido Bay. We carried our diving masks toward a stretch of rocky coastline a mile and a half away. At that windless, quiet hour the sea was glassy calm. It was so early that the pelicans hadn't begun their feeding yet. Then, about halfway to our destination, just a few feet to our left in shallow water against the shore, the smooth surface literally exploded. Over an area half the size of a tennis court, small waves suddenly appeared, and the water abruptly churned and foamed violently, with a sound like a roaring waterfall.

Ingrid was clearly and understandably frightened. "My God, Dad, what is it?" she asked as we stopped to watch from a safe distance.

"Feeding fish," I said. "I don't know what kind, but there sure are plenty of them. Look at that! Why didn't we bring a fishing rod along?"

Dozens of silver baitfish 4 to 6 inches long shot out of the water, sailing 3 feet and more in frenzied arcs, some of them beaching themselves in their panic. Looking closely, I could make out the gray backs of the feeding fish as they plowed at high speed through the baitfish schools.

After thirty or forty seconds, the ruckus stopped as quickly as it had begun. The ocean surface was glassy again, reflecting the orange sun that was just then rising over the dark mountains of Carmen Island. Ingrid spent a couple of minutes tossing stranded baitfish back into the water, and then we continued down the beach to do our diving.

I found out what we had seen later that day, when we visited Bill and Betty Rife, friends who have lived for several years in Loreto. As I described what had happened, Bill smiled. "Those were *toros*," he said. "I don't even know the English name for them, but they tend to feed along the shoreline, especially this time of year. I can tell you a pretty good story about them, too. Once when Betty and I were diving for lobsters in shallow water, all of a sudden we were engulfed in a cloud of baitfish—thousands of them—and the *toros* hit us right behind the baitfish. There were dozens of them, and they were actually bouncing off us in the water as they fed. The bad part came next. Pelicans were right behind the *toros*. When they started diving for the baitfish, we were really scared. Those are heavy birds, and they come down with enough speed and power to break a person's back. Luckily, everything had passed us by in a matter of seconds. But those *toros* are hot fish. Sometimes they'll go over ten pounds, occasionally a lot bigger, and they'll really take off for you. If you happen to get into a school of them with light tackle, I'll guarantee you you'll have some fun."

It sounded like some fun I wanted to have. Among the fishing and diving equipment I had brought along to Baja was an 8-foot fiberglass fly rod and a Hardy reel, an outfit I used back home in Oregon on trout streams. I rigged the little rod up that afternoon, with a bucktail streamer fly on 8-pound test at the business end. I also rigged a light spinning outfit with a silver spoon for Ingrid—but the days went by, and neither of us got a chance to fish in a school of feeding *toros*.

Whenever we took the rods with us on walks along the beach, the fish didn't show. Whenever we did see them feeding, we were heading out to sea in a boat with heavy tackle, or jogging empty-handed, or swimming back toward shore from diving. The problem was that their activity followed no discernible pattern of time or location. We saw them three or four times in the early morning, and as often in the heat of mid-afternoon. They appeared at random spots along the beach for a mile in either direction from our hotel, and their frenzied feeding never lasted for more than a minute or two in one place.

I did manage to learn a little more about *toros,* most of it from a young man named Steve who had come down to Baja from San Diego for yellowfin tuna fishing. On our fifth or sixth day, over Bohemia beers in the hotel bar, he told me what he knew. "Their English name is jack cravelle. I've never caught any either, but I've read about them. They herd schools of baitfish into shallow water, and then attack when they have them cornered. That's what you've been seeing. Sometimes they feed so hard they beach themselves. I've heard the biggest ones go over fifty pounds. At any size, they're supposed to be spectacular game fish. Who knows? Maybe they call them *toros* because they fight like bulls."

On our last morning, just before daybreak, I was standing on the second-floor balcony of our room, looking out across the beach at the smooth water 50 yards away. I had given up any hope of hooking a *toro,* and the light trout and spinning rods leaning in a corner of the room were all but forgotten.

Ingrid walked out onto the balcony to enjoy the view. "I think it's been the best ten days of my life," she said. "It's been a perfect vacation."

"It *has* been perfect," I agreed. I had hooked several tuna on my fly rod, and Ingrid had landed some good fish on trolling gear. We had watched schools of hundreds of porpoises playing, seen sea turtles, manta rays, and whales, dived for lobsters, visited astonishingly lovely, lonely beaches on offshore islands. Some Mexican friends had driven us out to a desert oasis for a feast of chocolate clams and *cabrilla,* or sea bass. To add to our pleasure there hadn't been so much as a single cloud in the summer sky for ten days.

"What time do we have to leave?" Ingrid asked me.

"The plane takes off at 11:55, so we ought to be out there an hour before that. We have plenty of time for a walk along the beach, or—"

Just then, when I was in mid-sentence, the *toros* appeared, directly across the beach from our room, and it was by far the largest school I'd seen. An area 20 yards long and extending at least 10 yards back from the shoreline erupted with their violent feeding, and the calm water churned and seethed with foam.

"My God!" said Ingrid. "There they are!"

I had already turned back into the room and grabbed the fly rod and two spare flies along with a pair of clippers from the writing table, and stuffed them into the back pocket of my shorts. Within seconds, I was on my way out the door. "Hurry up!" I called back to Ingrid.

"I don't even have my shoes on!"

"Hurry up!" I yelled again, running hard.

The busiest twenty minutes of my angling life followed. I sprinted down the stairs and around the corner, then along the passageway to the beach. When I hit the sand, the *toros* were still feeding, only 20 yards away now, and I stripped a few feet of line from the reel and began to false-cast it as I ran. The streamer fly hit the water near the very middle of the frothing waves and swirls created by the toros' feeding, and before I could even begin to retrieve line I had hooked a fish. The light rod bowed and a few yards of line were yanked from the reel, the fish running straight out to sea.

But the fly pulled out, the line went slack, and I quickly pulled the fly back into the *toros* again. Their frenzy had increased. Hundreds of baitfish were sailing through the air in all directions now. The roaring, rushing, hissing sound made by the *toros* as they plowed back and forth through the fish was exactly what you hear when you shoot through whitewater rapids in a kayak or raft.

30

I hooked another *toro* at once, as soon as the fly reached the edge of the feeding area. This fish ran the same way the first one had, but after 30 or 40 yards, the fly came away again.

I swore. In front of me, the feeding had abruptly stopped. I hadn't been setting the hook, I realized—and now it was too late. I swore harder. I'd finally had my chance, and I'd very stupidly blown it. Feeling frustrated and ridiculous, I cranked in the line that the second fish had run from the reel.

Then, about 50 yards out, I noticed small, rippling waves marking the calm surface, and moving steadily south, parallel with the beach. Their speed increased, and I knew it had to be the school of *toros,* cruising just beneath the surface after the baitfish. I ran down the beach after them, barely able to keep up, and after a quarter mile the school finally turned toward shore.

I was there to meet them. As soon as their feeding began, I dropped the fly into them again, and this time when the strike came I set the hook hard, three quick times in succession. The fish ran, 30, 40, 50 yards. "It can't be *that* big," I said to myself. "I'll stop him, turn him around, land him, and still have time to hook another one before the school moves off."

So I palmed the rim of the fly reel hard to stop the *toro.* I didn't stop him, though. This time, the fly broke off. By the time I'd reeled in my line, the school was gone again.

Again I saw the tell-tale ripples, about 40 yards out, moving north, back toward the hotel. As soon as I had knotted a new fly onto the leader tippet, I ran back after them. They went past the hotel, and finally swerved toward shore a couple of hundred yards beyond the place where I'd hooked the first two. I was panting by now, sweating hard.

This time nothing went wrong. I cast as soon as the feeding began, a *toro* struck the instant the fly touched water, and I set the hook and played this one carefully. Its first hard run, again straight to sea, went 80 or 90 yards. Just as the long run ended, Ingrid came up behind me with the spinning rod. The school was already gone, but still clearly visible, about 30 yards out, heading north.

"I could hear your reel all the way from the hotel," Ingrid said.

"See those ripples moving out there?" I told her. "Follow them, and when they head for shore get ready to cast. Just toss the spoon right into the middle of them!"

She set out running down the beach. My *toro* gave me four more strong, stubborn runs, and ten minutes later I finally slid it up the sandy beach. It weighed 10 or 12 pounds, and was blue-gray backed, silver-sided and white-bellied, deeply and powerfully built, and altogether lovely.

31

Then I looked for Ingrid and saw her a quarter mile to the north, standing at the waterline, with the bowed spinning rod glinting in the early-morning sunlight and the monofilament line visible, slanting at a long angle toward the *toro* she had hooked.

The *toro,* or jack cravelle, is an exciting game fish. All fish that feed close to shore are exciting, and—whether they are jacks, bluefish, striped bass, or amberjacks—if they are feeding you can usually catch them. In fact, the question in surf fishing isn't usually whether the fish are *hitting,* but whether they are *there.* Whether you are in Mexico or on Cape Cod, the best surf fishing spots are learned through trial and error and local knowledge, but there is always room for luck too. That is why, these days, I almost always carry a fishing rod with me when I'm anywhere near a beach.

I even carry one with me when I hike along the rocky coastline in Oregon, exploring tide pools. Tide-pool fishing is a relatively unknown and appealing form of angling. On old and inexpensive tackle, it is often easy to catch many fish in a short time. I generally use a fiberglass fly rod, a fast-sinking fly line, and a 4-foot leader of 12- or 15-pound test. A steelhead fly—number two or larger—works well in relatively clear water; spoons, spinners, or bait—mussels or strips of fish—are best when the water is murky.

An ideal tide pool is one that is large and deep, and that has a channel entering it from the open sea, even at low tide. If waves are flowing through it, so much the better. Even in pools not much larger than a bathtub, it's possible to catch rockfish that weights as much as 20 or 30 pounds. I know a fisherman who claims to have hauled a 50-pound cod out of such a pool. There are always small rockfish and surf perch, and these fish can be hooked on casts of 15 or 20 feet, or without casting at all. Sometimes it's simply a matter of lowering the bait or lure into the water. If you do try tide-pool fishing, though, take along extra tackle, because rockfish are very strong, heading for the bottom the instant they're hooked. Even with leaders of 20-pound test, you'll probably have to break off fairly often.

Sometimes, of course, it is necessary to cast considerable distances to reach feeding fish from shore, which is one reason why spin, bait, and surf-casting rods come in so many sizes. A long, powerful rod will throw a heavy lure or weight a long way. However, the same stiffness that makes long casts possible detracts considerably from the enjoyment of playing small- to moderate-sized fish, and also makes it somewhat more likely that a large fish will break off.

An angler limited to one outfit for fishing from shore can usually get by with a 9-foot spinning rod built with moderate action to cast weights of about 2 ounces. A well-made reel holding 200 yards of 20-pound-test line will handle most fish, but certainly not all of them. In any case, details of tackle have to be considered on a local basis. Fish with sharp teeth require wire leaders. Certain types, colors, and sizes of lures may be found to work best in specific areas and in narrowly-defined conditions that only local experts may recognize. There are places where schools of feeding fish will ignore lures on a high tide but will attack bait that is dragged along the pool's bottom. When the tide turns, these same fish may either leave the area or turn their attention to the surface, in which case popping bugs may be the only way to catch them. The speed of retrieve can be a crucial factor in your success. All of these considerations and many more will influence the choice of tackle you need.

Whatever tackle is used, once a fish is hooked from shore it must be landed by an angler standing in water, on sand, or on rocks. Fishermen who care about such things find this method much more challenging, and therefore more satisfying, than trolling or still-fishing from a boat.

Consider, for example, deep-sea fishing. Kip Farrington, a well-known angler, has said he believes that landing a large fish in deep water from a boat is 65 percent the skill of the captain, 20 percent the quality of the tackle, and only 15 percent the skill of the fisherman. If Farrington is anywhere near right —I happen to think he is—there would seem to be little reason to fish from a boat from a *sport*-fishing point of view. Landing a fish from shore, on the other hand, must be at least 75 percent the skill of the angler, and the rest the quality of his tackle.

And that is why I had no more than a passing interest in fishing from boats until, on a trip to Baja several years ago, I suffered probably the most frustrating angling experience of my life.

It was March, a month in which I had usually experienced good luck fishing from shore. I had several rods and reels with me, ranging from light fly tackle for jack cravelle to fairly heavy spinning gear for more distant targets.

Something strange happened that year—I didn't understand it then and I still don't. There were no fish feeding close to shore, not even in the deep water off rocky points. There were the usual schools of baitfish near shore—I could see them as I fished—but nothing was feeding on them. There were no jacks, no bonito or barracuda, no ladyfish or roosterfish, not even any pelicans.

For some reason, though, there was a great deal of feeding activity about 150 yards offshore. Out there, well beyond my longest cast with any tackle,

I could see clouds of baitfish leaping from the water. Behind the baitfish were the swirls and wakes of the large fish chasing after them. A couple of times I saw the dorsal fins of roosterfish cutting through the calm water as they fed on the surface. Still nothing ever came close to shore. Day after frustrating day, in one spot after another, I tried to reach the action, but I couldn't. I waited for the action to come to me, but it never did. I was reminded of my days as a young man in New York City, when I walked the streets without enough money in my pocket for food and my stomach knotted with hunger, as I gazed into restaurant windows where diners sat enjoying their elaborate meals.

It was a week-long trip, but after five days of suffering I gave it up. On my sixth morning, I got out of bed, drank a cup of coffee, and convinced myself that there was more to life than fishing, even in Baja.

I put on an old pair of shorts and some running shoes and jogged a couple of miles down the beach, watching the feeding fish out where they had been all week, well beyond my reach. After a couple of miles, I cut west along a dusty, rutted road toward the dark outlines of the Sierra de la Giganta Mountains. Immediately I was glad to be away from the ocean and all its disappointments.

In a narrow lagoon off to my right a small flock of bluebill ducks lifted off the water when they saw me coming, then banked steeply in flight and circled back toward the beach. One hundred yards beyond the lagoon a large covey of quail rocketed out of the sagebrush just a few feet off the edge of the road, startling me, as the whirring wings of upland birds always do. Though I could hear several species of songbird in the gum and mesquite trees, none were in sight so early in the day.

I crossed the Baja Highway—not with a car in sight in either direction —and picked up my pace. I was feeling better, very good in fact, without a fishing rod in my hand. The road became a trail, studded with rocks and boulders which *chubascos* had washed down a steep arroyo just a few yards to my right. Then, when I ran up a short, steep hill and started down the other side, I saw the roadrunner. It was 30 yards in front of me, at the side of the trail between two clumps of sage, looking back at me over its shoulder.

I stopped in my tracks and blinked, then stared. The bird stood motionless, staring back. There was no mistaking it. I was surprised at how much this genuine roadrunner looked like the one in the Saturday-morning cartoons. Nearly 2 feet tall, it had a bluish crown, a patch of red behind its eyes, a brown-and-white-mottled back, and a long, white-tipped tail. Its long legs were strong-looking, the four-toed feet large. There was even more to the

34

similarity. In its stance, the gleam in its eye, and the way it stood there looking back at me with its head cocked slightly to one side, this roadrunner had the unmistakable aura of a wise-ass.

I thought about it. I was warmed up, feeling strong and confident. I was also terribly frustrated at five days straight of not catching anything. So, why not catch a roadrunner? I knew that they seldom flew, and that they were capable of ground speeds of up to 20 miles per hour, but I doubted that they could hold such a speed for long. This was rough country, but vegetation was sparse enough that I would be able to keep the bird in sight, even if he opened up a temporary lead of 80 or 100 yards. There was no chance I could actually catch the bird, or even touch it—nor would I have wanted to, given the fact that they are capable of killing rattlesnakes—but perhaps I could make it fly. That would be enough, I decided. I felt that making a roadrunner fly would constitute an indignity for the bird, in my mind if not in his. More importantly, I would prove to myself that I could meet a challenge on land if not on sea.

Probably five seconds had passed by the time I had made a commitment to action, and I used another five to plot my strategy. It occurred to me that all conditions suggested a hard, sudden sprint. The just-risen sun was directly behind me. It was downhill all the way from me to the bird. I had the element of surprise on my side, too. It was very possible, even quite likely, that this roadrunner had never seen a human being before, and it had surely never known one to come straight at it, at full speed, first thing in the morning. With luck, I could end this chase in a hurry.

I took a deep breath, and, screaming and waving my arms wildly, charged down the hill. I was halfway to the roadrunner, no more than 15 yards away, and it hadn't moved a feather. I was 10 yards away. Its dark eyes glittered in the morning light. I thought I saw its long body tense, then lean slightly forward. It turned its head when I was 5 short yards away.

Very suddenly, without my even having seen it move, the roadrunner was gone. The situation was very much like a cartoon. At my feet, where the bird had been, was a small, slowly-settling cloud of fine brown dust. About 30 yards ahead, streaking through the sagebrush and cactus plants alongside the trail, was a brownish blur—and by the time I had judged the distance between us to be 30 yards, the bird had nearly doubled it.

I started after him, not in a sprint, but at a pace I thought I could hold for a good half mile. Within seconds I was conscious of my own labored breathing, and the sound of my feet pounding hard against the sun-baked earth. I kicked a stone with my right foot and swore in pain.

The roadrunner stayed close beside the trail, occasionally swerving around a clump of sage or the trunk of a saguaro cactus. He was an impressive runner all right—stiff-legged and erect, leaning slightly forward—and about half a minute after I started my pursuit, I heard him call. He didn't say "Beep beep!" though. He sounded more like a cooing dove, if somewhat louder and deeper. Both his running posture and the call, delivered half a dozen times, seemed to me to convey his cockiness.

Nevertheless, within half a minute's time I had cut the distance between us in half. Then, he stopped abruptly and looked back at me again. "Maybe he is finished," I thought. It could be that roadrunners were the 60-meter-dash runners of the avian world.

By now we were on level ground, and I tried another sprint, straight at him. I was 30 yards away, then 20. Then he started off again, did a quick left turn, crossed the trail, and ran through some flowering cactus plants with sword-like leaves.

I slowed my pace again and followed. Off the trail the earth was sandy, making it harder to run. Already I was sweating hard and panting for breath, but I managed to close the distance again. I also managed to cut my right arm, just below the elbow, on one of the cactus plants. I swore again and kept on running.

The roadrunner, dodging around sagebrush, rocks, and cactus, varied his speed but never stopped again. He made a long, gradual right-hand turn that became a full circle and brought us back to the trail at the same place we had left it.

Though far from exhausted, I was growing tired. When you run through rough country it usually isn't the distance that takes it out of you as much as it is the road's twists and turns and your constant adjustments in stride. Compounding my particular problem was my having to concentrate on two things at once—the roadrunner up ahead, and the ground directly in front of my feet. This was no place to trip and fall.

The roadrunner crossed the trail, then disappeared down into the arroyo. When I jogged to the edge and looked in, I saw him perched on a boulder 15 yards away. I should have given up then. The arroyo was at least 10 feet deep and 20 feet across in places, and some of the boulders dotting its floor were the size of cars. They had washed down from the steep mountain slopes during the violent storms that sometimes hit Baja in late summer and early fall. There had to be rattlesnakes down there, and it was a place where a *human* runner could easily take a brutal spill.

Looking straight into my eyes, the roadrunner seemed as arrogant as ever.

I thought of all the fish I hadn't caught again. Then, when I started down after him, a quick-legged lizard dashed across a pile of small rocks at my feet, so startling me that I jumped. Then the roadrunner called again, cooing ten or a dozen times. Before I got anywhere near him, he hopped to the next large boulder up the arroyo. He hopped at least 10 feet, without apparent effort—but he didn't fly.

The next few minutes would have made an excellent cartoon. The roadrunner stayed in the arroyo, hopping from boulder to boulder, heading toward the mountains about half a mile away. Whenever I climbed down into the arroyo, he hopped away ahead of me, and there was no way I could keep up. Whenever I climbed back out of the arroyo, the roadrunner sat there looking at me from a rock. I climbed in and out several times, always with the same result, and all I got for my trouble was the fall I'd been worried about, and a bloody scrape just below my left knee.

After the fall, I knew I'd had enough. My right big toe was bruised and sore from the rock I'd kicked, and my right arm and left leg were bleeding. I was soaked with sweat and coated with dust. The roadrunner, the last time I looked at him, was up in the arroyo, perched atop yet another boulder a good 40 yards away and looking back at me, none the worse for wear.

I turned around and jogged back the way I'd come.

I spent the rest of the day casting flies and lures toward feeding fish. As usual, I couldn't reach the action and I didn't hook a thing.

The next day I started for home, and one of the very first things I did once back in Oregon was to convince Hilde we needed a boat.

37

Fishing from a Small Boat

Buying a small fishing boat isn't quite as simple a matter as it might appear, because there are dozens of models, makes, and materials from which to choose. Several considerations apply when choosing one boat over all the others available. For example, how far and how fast will you need to travel? Will you be trolling most of the time, or still-fishing, or casting? How rough and windy is the ocean in the area you want to fish? Will you have to transport the boat long distances, and if so, over what kind of country? Will there be launching facilities when you get there? Obviously, cost is relevant to all of these considerations. Even small boats can cost a great deal of money these days.

With all of these considerations in mind, I (personally) chose a very modest boat indeed—but it was one I felt would serve its purpose perfectly. Through a mail order catalogue, I purchased a twelve-foot inflatable for about $500. For another $750 I bought a six-horsepower outboard motor, which was the largest size recommended for the inflatable. Such a boat and motor would be useless for ocean fishing in most places. It certainly wouldn't have done me much good on the Oregon coast near my home. But my wife Hilde and I were going to fish in the area of Puerto Escondido, a few miles south of Loreto (the scene of my frustrations while casting from shore).

"Puerto Escondido" translates into "Hidden Bay", and it is a name well-chosen. In fact, Escondido is known as the calmest area in the Sea of Cortez. During hurricane season—August and September—yachts from hundreds of miles around congregate in Escondido for the safety it affords. Escondido is also known as an area in which several species of fish can be found near shore, so Hilde and I doubted we would ever feel a need to travel more than 2 or 3 miles from the coastline to get all the sport we wanted. We would troll flies and feather lures and stop the boat to cast when conditions were right for it.

We planned to spend the month of November in Escondido, and I bought both the boat and the motor a couple of months ahead. When the boat arrived, we spent an afternoon assembling it in the back yard. A week later, we went for an inaugural cruise on a nearby mountain lake, and in three hours got the feel of the boat and broke in the motor. After three more lake trips, we felt we were ready. Everything seemed familiar and everything worked well.

Toward the end of October, we left Ashland on a typically gray and rainy day and headed south with the boat, the motor, and all our camping gear and fishing tackle packed into our station wagon.

Five days later, Hilde hooked the first fish of our trip. After a smooth journey down Interstate 5 through California, and then along the lovely Baja Highway, we arrived at Escondido on a warm Saturday afternoon. It took only a couple of hours to get set up in the campground there, and another thirty minutes to put the boat and motor together. With a good hour of daylight left, we couldn't resist trying them out, so we cruised through the narrow entrance to the bay, then turned south to troll along the coast. I had taken only enough time to rig one rod, for Hilde. It was a 9-foot fly rod with a Fin Nor reel, and a large white bucktail streamer on a 15-pound-test leader. No more than five minutes after we started she had her first strike, but the fish was gone before she had a chance to get excited.

"I didn't think anything would happen so fast," she said.

"I have a feeling you'll get one," I said. "Just wait."

No sooner had I said that than another fish hit hard. I cut the motor, and the fish ran out at least 80 yards of line. I smiled at the look of shocked surprise on Hilde's face.

A few minutes later she landed a 10-pound sierra, a handsome silver mackerel with golden dots along its sides. We killed it for that night's dinner and the next day's lunch, then turned back toward the bay. Halfway back another sierra struck, and as soon as I cut the motor Hilde handed me the rod to let me land the catch. We released this one—I was careful about the sharp teeth when I took the hook out—and arrived back at the harbor well before sunset. I anchored the boat in 4 feet of water, just inshore from where several big yachts were moored, and we went back to camp for our sierra dinner. Our month in a small boat had begun quite well.

That night, in the shower room shared by campers and the owners and crews of yachts, a young man asked me if I was from one of the boats in the bay. "People start to show up for the winter in November," he explained, "and it's hard to keep track of them all."

"My wife and I have a boat down here," I said. "How about you?"

"We got in last week on the *Tropical Star.*"

"Where from?"

"Northern California."

"Must be a good-sized boat."

"About 40 tons," he answered.

"Ours isn't quite that big," I said.

Our boat and motor together weighed 147 pounds. We named it the *Zucarita,* which is the Spanish word for Sugar-Frosted Flakes™, and translates into "little sugar."

We chose that name because it was with Zucaritas that we began our routine every morning for the entire month. I have a very reliable internal clock when it comes to fishing, and I awoke each morning within minutes of half-past five. I rolled out of the sleeping bag, awakened Hilde, then put a pot of coffee water on the camp stove. We ate our Zucaritas first, along with cups of Tang, then sat on camp chairs outside the tent to watch the sun rise, with cups of coffee sweetened with Kahlua.

After two cups each we loaded the back of the station wagon with our fishing rods and tackle, the gas tank, diving masks, tools, boat-patching materials, an air pump, first aid supplies, an ice chest, oars, life preservers, and two folding chairs. By 6:30 A.M. we were headed for the bay, about half a mile from the campground. It took no more than five minutes to load the boat, the two chairs facing each other at opposite ends, the ice chest in the middle, the gas tank and other gear secured beneath the chairs. By 6:45 we were heading out the narrow entrance to the bay, with nothing but up to six hours of fishing ahead of us.

It was even more fun than I had imagined it would be. We learned something every day, and every day something unexpected happened. We fished the shallow waters along shore, the deep blue water offshore, and the drop-offs and ledges near the offshore islands. We trolled at about 6 miles per hour, sometimes a little faster, using flies and lures that I had made myself back in Oregon. Hilde had a 9-foot graphite fly rod, and her Fin Nor reel held 300 yards of line. I used my 9-foot fiberglass steelhead rod with a Hardy Sunbeam loaded with 400 yards of line. My drag was much lighter, and the extra hundred yards of line was insurance against a large fish taking the whole reel. Our line was 30-pound-test Dacron™, our leaders 15-pound-test monofilament, (sometimes ten). We also carried an extra fly rod, so that we could cast to fish when a good opportunity presented itself.

Escondido, like any well-known fishing area, had its resident experts. We met Americans who had been spending the winters there for fifteen years, and Mexicans who had spent their entire lives fishing there. We heard their various theories concerning trolling speeds, the best baits and lures, the best spots to fish, the right tackle, the most productive times of day. I listened carefully to all of the advice we heard, and I also ignored much of it. I'm sure that all of it was well-intentioned, and that most of it was quite reliable, but I wanted to discover things on my own. We had plenty of time, and because of that luxury we didn't have to care about catching a great number of fish every day. I was certain that we would catch our share, and that if we did things our own way at least part of the time we would learn much about small-boat fishing in the process.

I made notes after each day's fishing, and to convey what our month was like, I'll share accounts of a few of those days with you here:

Day One We went two and a half miles out to Danzante Island and trolled along its western shore. The water was perfectly smooth, and just off the north tip of the island I thought I saw slight surface disturbances. When we swung by that area Hilde's rod bowed violently, and a large fish thrashed on the surface 25 yards behind the boat and ran out 10 or 15 yards of line. But then it turned and swam straight toward us, its tail cutting through the water.

"Reel!" I said to Hilde. "As fast as you can!"

She was reeling already, but it didn't help. Before she could get the line tightened, the fish was off.

"Dorado," I said.

"For sure?"

"Nothing else stays on top that way. It was a big one, too."

We trolled the area for ten minutes, circling and criss-crossing without result. We were using white-and-yellow flies, and when they failed to produce another strike we reeled in and changed to homemade lures: a blue-and-white squid for Hilde and a red-and-white model for me. I was anxious to try these, especially for dorado. A few weeks before leaving Oregon I had noticed packages of vinyl squids for sale in the sporting goods department of a discount store. A dozen sold for about $2, and I bought several packages, thinking that at that price I could hardly go wrong. After some thought I decided to use very large fly hooks on them and combine the squids with red-and-white hackle feathers to create a sort of combination feather lure and streamer fly. They were between 4 and 5 inches long—big enough for large fish—and they looked just fine in the tackle box. When we dropped them over the side to let out line, they looked good in the water, too. But we didn't hook another dorado.

We trolled around three small islands south of Danzante, and missed

42

several strikes. Then we headed for the mainland, to troll the lovely, lonely coast back to the bay. Not long after we hit shallow water where we could easily see the bottom, Hilde hooked, landed, and released a 6-pound jack cravelle.

Minutes after that, she hooked what we assumed was a bonito of 3 or 4 pounds. Within minutes she had it up close to the boat. Then, suddenly, line began to race from the reel, faster and faster. Fifty yards were gone, then 100, then 150, all within what seemed like a very few seconds. Then, just as suddenly as it had begun, the long run stopped, and Hilde reeled in the bonito. It was dead. Something had crushed it nearly flat. It couldn't have been a shark, because a shark's teeth would have cut through its flesh. A very large dorado? A yellowtail? A roosterfish? We'll never know.

I used a filleting knife to cut a strip of meat from what was left of the bonito. The strip was 6 inches long and 1 inch wide and included the skin. I replaced my squid with a bait hook, and then trolled very slowly with the strip of bonito, using at least fifty yards of line out behind the boat—twice as much as we had been using with the artificial lures.

Before we'd gone 50 yards something struck the strip bait hard, but I missed the fish, and when I reeled in the bait was gone. I realized that to prevent that happening in the future, I'd have to put on two hooks, one of them near the rear end of the bait.

On our way back to Escondido we hooked and released three more jack cravelle.

Day Four   Weather still warm and very calm. As soon as we left the bay we saw a school of porpoises, and I chased after them and finally caught up. They rolled all around us for several minutes, and one stayed just a few feet ahead of the boat, leaping out of the water for us four or five times.

When the porpoises outdistanced us, we turned north to troll along the rocky cliffs there. In an hour we hooked and released a large bonito and a needlefish. With the sun high and bright over the mountains, we turned out toward deeper water, to fish the channel between Danzante and the bay.

After half an hour without a strike, my reel was suddenly screeching with the run of a powerful fish. I cut the motor and looked back in time to see a dorado 3 feet over the water, writhing in the sunlight.

"I have one too!" Hilde yelled, and just as she said it another dorado jumped near mine.

For a while the *Zucarita* was a lively place. Each fish jumped ten or a dozen times, and we had to change sides in the boat nearly that often. When I had

43

my fish near the boat—its sides flashing green and golden, its pectoral fins a luminescent blue—I saw that two more dorado were following in after the hooked one.

"Land yours," I said to Hilde, "and I'll keep mine in the water. Maybe we can catch the other ones."

Hilde landed hers, and then I handed her my rod, grabbed the extra rod, and began to work line out for a short cast. The two dorado were still there, swimming in circles around the hooked one. When the streamer fly hit the water I twitched it twice, and the nearest dorado started at it hard. He couldn't have been more than 6 inches short of the fly when he stopped abruptly, then turned and swam away out of sight. The other followed. I tried a few more casts, but neither fish reappeared, so we landed the second hooked fish.

Schooled dorado will often follow a hooked fish toward a boat. My mistake had been to bring the hooked fish in too close. We had been in plain view, and that had undoubtedly spooked them. Next time I would keep the hooked fish 40 or 50 feet away instead of twenty.

About a mile from the bay, we hooked a ladyfish over a shallow, sandy stretch of bottom. I pulled the boat to shore and anchored it. While Hilde collected shells, I cast small white flies for the ladyfish and landed and released eight or ten of them. The school finally moved off. It was after 1:00 when we got back to shore.

Day Seven When two people troll a calm sea in a small boat with a quiet motor there is bound to be a great deal of conversation. Hilde and I had talked of many things, but mostly of fishing, and we had agreed that we each wanted more than anything else to hook a large dorado by the end of our month. "Large" to us meant 20 pounds. On our tackle, though, even 15 pounds would qualify.

We had also come to realize exactly what we liked about light-tackle fishing from a small boat. For one thing, we appreciated its simplicity. Because we were never more than a couple of miles from the mainland or an offshore island, and because there were always other boats reasonably nearby, we didn't need a radio or an extra motor. If our motor died I might have to paddle for a few hours, and if a sudden storm came up we might have to spend an afternoon or even a night on a beach somewhere. But this was unlikely. Our principal worry was where to fish, but that wasn't really a problem either, because we caught fish of some kind nearly everywhere we went. As we talked, and enjoyed the clear skies, the steep mountains, the rocky cliffs, the miles of deserted beach, and the clear water all around us, there was plenty of fishing action.

Hilde held her rod out the right-hand side of the boat, and I faced her across the ice chest, with my left arm handling the motor, and holding my rod across my lap out the left side. The rods were light enough so that holding them that way for a few hours at a stretch was no problem. I've always felt that the most exciting moments in fishing are missed if the rod is in a holder: the strike itself and the first hard run of a fish, or its first wild jumps from the water.

We certainly enjoyed the independence of having our own boat. Whenever we felt like it, we were free to cut the motor and simply drift in lovely silence for a while, watching birds, porpoises, seals, or whales. Or, we could stop on an island to have lunch and explore a beach, and if it was a hot day, pull on our diving masks and swim with dozens of species of brightly marked fish in a sheltered lagoon.

Something else I thoroughly appreciated was the fact that it was my responsibility to find fish, not theirs to find me. Though it was possible to hook something through blind luck nearly anywhere, I soon learned that the time of day, the cloud cover, the tide, and the wind affected the fishing. Certain areas proved to be best for hooking certain species. It also became evident that different species were attracted to different colors and sizes of flies and lures. I learned to watch the surface closely far ahead of the boat, and I learned to intercept moving schools of feeding fish. Sometimes, pelicans and frigatebirds showed us where the feeding was going on. It was satisfying to see pieces of the puzzle fall into place day by day.

One discovery we made on the seventh day concerned wahoo. I had heard rumors that schools of these large, ferocious fish were in the area, but hooking one seemed a very remote possibility.

We had started out a little earlier than usual, because we wanted to troll in front of the Escondido pier before anyone else began fishing from it. The day before, several 10-pound dorado and an even larger roosterfish had been caught on live bait from the pier. Perhaps, if some good fish were still out there, one or two of them would accept our trolled squids.

Hilde was using a blue-and-white model, and I a red-and-white one. We swung back and forth in front of the pier three or four times without a strike. On our last pass, I saw a small cloud of silver baitfish explode from the water about 200 yards away, out near the lighthouse. A very large fish weighing at least 30 pounds slashed out of the water behind the baitfish. Then two more big fish showed, and I immediately turned in their direction, revving the motor up as high as it could go.

When we were halfway to where the fish were, the large one showed again, in the same area. By now I thought that they were 40-pounders. It's difficult to distinguish colors in morning light, but these fish appeared to be bright silver, with vertical bars down their sides. They were long and slender, with pointed snouts. Except for their vertical bars, they looked like giant-sized sierra.

We soon reached the area, and slowed to trolling speed. I held the *Zucarita* about 20 yards from the rocky coastline, just over a drop-off. Over the left side of the boat, I could see the rocky bottom some 30 feet down. Over the right side, the sea was deep and blue.

Just a few seconds after we'd slowed, Hilde had a hard strike. Her rod tip was yanked halfway down into the water. "God!" she said. "That was something big!"

"I could tell."

After a minute or two I made a wide circle and started back. Over the same area—the same spot, it seemed to me—both rods then bowed at once, line racing from their reels. I cut the motor, but within seconds the line stopped racing and went dead.

"What happened?" Hilde asked.

"They're just gone."

"But why?"

"I think it's my fault." I was furious at myself. "Last night I tied our knots in the dark with a flashlight. Remember? I must have tied bad knots. There's no other way we could lose two fish at once like that."

"They were both hooked."

"I know it."

We had been reeling in as we talked, and I examined the lines. There was no sign that either squid had broken off at the knot. The lines appeared to have been severed very cleanly, as if with a sharp knife. "Maybe it *wasn't* my fault," I said.

I very carefully tied on two more of the squids, testing them by pulling at the knots with all my strength. Then we started up, let out line, made another turn, and went back over the hot spot.

Both rods bowed again. Line raced from the reels again. I cut the motor and turned in time to see Hilde's fish jump—long, slender, at least 40 pounds, its vertical bars clear from that distance—and then both rods again went dead.

I swore as creatively as I have in years. We reeled in, and discovered that once more both lines had been neatly severed.

"They're wahoo," I said, "and I never knew they had such sharp teeth."

A few minutes later we had another double hook-up. Hilde's fish got away as the others had done, but this time mine stayed on. It must have been hooked through its lip, the leader safe from its teeth.

It was a powerful fish, but after its first long runs I was fairly sure I'd be able to handle it and eventually get it back to the boat. Then, as I was slowly regaining line, there was a sudden yank at the rod unlike anything I'd ever felt from a hooked fish, and the wahoo was gone.

I reeled in, and found that this time the line had been severed 5 feet up from the squid. Wahoos are known to hit anything that shines, and one had apparently struck at the brass swivel that joined the Dacron™ line and the monofilament leader.

"Wahoo fishermen need *wire* leaders," I said. "That's the lesson for today."

Day Eleven   It was too windy to fish offshore, so we had no choice but to troll south within 50 yards of the coast in fairly shallow water and hope for sierra, roosterfish, or jack cravelle. We went nearly two hours without a strike, and because the first couple of hours are usually the most productive, I resigned myself to a slow day.

We had changed flies several times, and tried various color combinations on our squids. When we approached two cliffs with about 30 yards of sandy beach between them, I was using a red-and-yellow bucktail streamer fly and Hilde had gone back to a blue-and-white squid.

Rocky cliffs are almost always good spots for cabrilla, because over the centuries earthquakes and erosion have toppled boulders into the sea, making cover for rockfish and attracting schools of baitfish as well.

The water was fairly choppy, but I could see well enough to spot dangerous underwater rocks before we reached them, so I trolled as close to the cliffs as I could get. The water's depth ranged from 4 to 12 feet. As I passed by the sandy beach I saw baitfish 20 yards ahead of us.

"Get ready," I said to Hilde. "Something's feeding in here."

Just as we passed the second cliff, her rod tip was yanked down hard. "I missed it," she said, but before she had the words out another fish hit, and this one hooked itself. For safety's sake, I took us out 20 yards to sea, away from the rocks, before I cut the motor. When I did, Hilde's fish had just stopped its first long run. More than 100 yards of line was out, and it took her five minutes to work the powerful, stubborn fish close to the boat. When the fish was close enough to see the boat, it began to circle us, and at that point Hilde could gain no more line. "It's strong," she said. "What is it?"

"I can see it now. A jack cravelle. A good one, too."

It was an 8-pound fish, and Hilde hooked, landed, and released seven more just like it that morning. I didn't hook a single one—I didn't have a strike from one—but for the sake of experiment, I didn't switch to a blue-and-white squid. This experience was the clearest proof I've ever had that even furiously-feeding fish have definite color preferences. For half an hour, every time we trolled by those cliffs, Hilde hooked a jack. All the flies I tried—combinations of red, yellow, white, and orange—were ignored.

After half an hour the jacks moved on, but were replaced by a school of ladyfish which fed over the sand between the cliffs. They weren't as particular, and, for the next half hour, we had one double hook-up after another. These were 3-pound fish, and though they didn't run away from the strike with the power of jacks, they were spectacular jumpers. Some of them left the water half a dozen times as we worked them in.

Day Twelve   We went back to the cliffs. Again it was too windy and choppy to fish deep water.

The jacks were back, and this time we both used blue-and-white squids. All morning long, we hooked a fish or two each time we trolled by the cliffs. The wind picked up at 10:00, and our little boat was getting tossed around. Playing fish and handling the motor at the same time wasn't easy. After a while, I stopped fishing. It wasn't a dangerous situation, just uncomfortable, but we finally decided we'd head back to Escondido as soon as we had trolled all the way alongside both cliffs without Hilde hooking a fish.

We couldn't do it. Wind was gusting hard from the north and swells were rolling in from the same direction, and the jacks kept hitting. Finally, after more hooked fish than I could keep track of, we headed back. Neither of us bothered to fish along the way. We were afraid we might hook something.

Day Sixteen   The wind had died, and the sea flattened out again. We trolled north along shore for half a mile, but there were no signs of fish, so we swung out to deep water and headed south, toward two small islands a couple of miles away.

We had almost reached the first of the islands when something struck my squid, but missed it. A few seconds later there was another, harder strike, and this time the fish was hooked. I cut the motor and watched the line melt from my reel. It was either a tuna or a large bonito, and it headed straight for the bottom, not with great speed, but with steady, unstoppable power.

It took fifteen minutes to land this 20-pound skipjack tuna. I admired it for a few seconds, then twisted the hook from the corner of its jaw and dropped both the fish and my red-and-white squid back into the water.

I started up the motor and began to strip line from my reel, but before the squid was 30 feet behind the boat a dorado struck it. Dorado have two ways of striking. Some of them simply stop the lure, and when you first feel such a fish it's impossible to tell what or how big it is. Then it jumps, sometimes two or three times, and takes off on its first long run. In contrast, other dorado hit a lure or bait at full speed, which probably means they saw it from a long way off and raced to get it. This kind of strike is almost frightening. I don't think any other fish can shatter the calm of the Sea of Cortez like a hard-hitting dorado.

This particular fish had 50 yards of line out before I could even begin to react. When I cut the motor and turned to look, all I saw was a very quickly-travelling wake going away from the boat, at a slight angle to my left, toward shore. It went another 50 yards or more that way, perhaps an inch underwater, and it finally jumped, throwing spray in all directions. I saw the hook fly away when it threw it. It dropped back to the surface ahead of the fish. Then the dorado hit flat on its side with a splat that sounded like a gunshot, and suddenly the sea was calm again. It was the first really good-sized dorado we had hooked on the trip—more than 15 pounds.

I sat there feeling stupid and helpless. "I didn't even have my line out," I said to Hilde.

"I know you didn't."

"The drag wasn't even tightened up, that's why he didn't get hooked."

"Maybe there'll be more."

"Maybe," I said. "But we won't get too many chances like that."

I was very wrong about that. A few minutes later we reached the island, which was about 150 yards long and half as wide. It consisted of two rocky hills thick with cactus, one hill twice as large as the other. They were connected by a narrow arm of land that now, at high tide, was nearly underwater. The western edge of the island—the smaller of the two hills—was no more than 300 yards from shore, and the water around it ranged from 20 to 40 feet deep. The bottom was mostly white sand, but had several large boulders showing.

When we began to troll around the island, I hoped for a cabrilla or two, or perhaps another school of jack cravelle. Then, just off the island's lower tip, another dorado struck. It too hit the squid at full speed and kept right on going, straight toward shore. When I cut the motor and turned I could actually see the fish, its back and tail out of water, speeding away, with the leader cutting the surface cleanly. Then, like the first one, the dorado jumped and threw the hook. Very suddenly, the rod went dead in my hand.

"Two in a row. That one was even *bigger*."

Hilde smiled, and, as usual, took the optimistic view. "Maybe there'll be even more," she said.

"If there are, I hope *you* hook them," I answered. "I can't do it right."

But that day, the luck was all mine. I hooked seven dorado trolling around that island, all of them good ones. For more than half an hour, every time I started up the motor, another one was there. They ignored Hilde's blue-and-white squid. They hit my red-and-white one as hard as any fish ever hit anything. I actually landed only two of the fish, but the last one was exactly what I wanted: a twenty-pounder that never stopped running and jumping for a quarter of an hour.

When we headed back in, I told Hilde I wouldn't complain if I didn't hook another fish for the rest of the month. I meant it, too. I hoped it was her turn.

Day Twenty-One   The weather was perfect again, and we went to the small island, but the dorado had left the area—or, if they hadn't left, they had stopped striking.

Nevertheless, we had an experience that typifies one of the strong attractions of the Escondido area. Trolling up and down the shallow channel between the island's western tip and the mainland, we hooked six good fish of six different species in less than an hour: a dog snapper, a roosterfish, a cabrilla, a jack cravelle, a sierra, and a bonito. In this so-called midriff section of the Sea of Cortez, you truly never know what you will hook or how big it will be.

Later in the morning, on the way back to the bay, Hilde had a strike from what had to be a large dorado. Her rod, held at a right angle to the boat, was yanked so hard that it swung over my head and knocked my hat off. A second later, I saw the sudden disappointment on her face when she realized the fish was gone. "I could barely get the rod over your head," she said. "That was a big one!"

"It had to be a dorado. Nothing else hits that hard and runs off at an angle that way."

"I doubt if I'll ever catch one."

"You will. We have time. I'll rig up that ten-foot graphite rod for you tomorrow."

"What difference will that make?"

"Changing something you fish with can change your luck. That's why I brought three hats down here. I wear one as long as the fishing stays good, but as soon as I have a slow day I switch to another one. It works, too—almost always."

Hilde laughed, but I was serious. No one knows why, but confidence has a lot to do with successful fishing. The people who think they're going to catch fish usually do, and the people who don't think they're going to catch fish usually don't. I've found that changing rods, reels, lures, lines, or even hats can sometimes instill enough confidence to make a difference. Someday, perhaps, a patient researcher will explain this by proving that fish have some mysterious sense that is attuned to the moods of the people who try to catch them.

So, after lunch, I took Hilde's reel off the 9-foot rod she had been using and put it on our 10-footer. Then, something happened that gave Hilde's confidence a definite boost. When we went to shop in the little grocery store near the campground, we noticed a display of lures for sale. The sign read:

CORTEZ LURES
made especially for Escondido Bay

Four different lures were displayed, one of which was called a "Willie Wonder." To our great surprise, the Willie Wonder was the very same blue-and-white vinyl squid that Hilde had been using. There was some small print beneath the Willie Wonders on the rack:

especially for dorado, to be trolled at 8 to 10 mph about 20 yards behind the boat

I was never able to find out who made these lures. The vinyl squids are manufactured in Kent, Washington, so it's not unlikely they came from a Pacific Northwest salmon fisherman who retired in Baja.

"So I've been fishing with a Willie Wonder all along," Hilde said.

"Sure. And they're especially for dorado. You can't miss now. Tomorrow's the day."

Day Twenty-Two   I woke up half an hour earlier than usual. Outside the tent window the stars were bright in a moonless sky. There was no trace of wind through the leaves of the bougainvillea bushes, which meant that it would almost surely be a calm day. Dew covered the grass, and that was another indication of stable weather.

Before waking Hilde, I put water on the camp stove for coffee, dressed,

51

made the coffee, and added a spoonful of Kahlua. Then I sat in a camp chair and picked up one of the several books we had brought along, Ray Cannon's *The Sea of Cortez*. With the help of a flashlight, I leafed through pages until I found the section on dorado. It's entitled "The Finest Game Fish of All," and, as I sipped the strong, hot coffee, I read it through for perhaps the tenth time:

If asked what was the most enthralling thing I have seen in the Cortez, I would have to sift through a thousand exciting incidents. But if I were to choose the one that stimulated the greatest number of head-to-heel emotions, I would select the time I saw a school of about a hundred dolphinfish rainbowing up in unison for a 50-foot-long leap. They formed a high continuous arch of much splendor. The last, sharp rays of a setting sun had caught the vaulters and intensified the brilliant colors.

There seems to be no satisfying the ravenous appetite of dolphinfish. I have seen them snatch baits just a few inches in front of the noses of big sharks and billfish. At first sight of a tabogganing bait, this voracious creature, like the needlefish, often takes off from a great distance and comes bounding through the air, or rips the surface for a hundred yards to be first at a morsel. When hooked, it bounds as high as 15 feet. I know of no other 50- to 75-pound swimmer that will hit a lure trolled at 20 knots and pass the boat before the angler can feel the strike, then keep the rod in the form of a question mark for an hour and a half.

Add to this all the hocus-pocus tricks this protean showoff uses to flamboozle a fisherman: a hundred-yard peel-off straight away, then a sudden reversal right toward the boat; quick, unexpected slips under the craft, across its bow, then under and up near the outboard prop. Finally, if all else fails to dislodge the hook, the creature will possum until the over-confident angler relaxes the line, then spit the hook out right in front of the premature victor. It is no wonder that most saltwater angling authorities say that no other fish of all the oceans can match the many qualities of *el dorado,* "the finest game fish of them all."

I closed the book and put it back, finished the coffee, and then shook Hilde by the shoulder. "Come on," I said. "It's time to get up. This is the day."

Sure enough, it was.

We began by trolling north, along the coast toward an island at the western entrance of Juancalito Bay. I had a hunch—one of those strong feelings based on nothing but instinct, but which I've learned to trust—that we would find dorado in that direction.

Half an hour out of Escondido, I hooked a skipjack tuna. I could tell what it was at once by the way it took line out and down in strong bursts of 30 to 40 yards at a time, until it reached the bottom. After ten minutes, just as I had begun to work the fish back up, the hook pulled away.

"What are you using?" Hilde asked me as I reeled in.

"Same as usual, the red-and-white squid. Maybe you should change to that."

She thought about it. "No. I'll stick with blue-and-white."

"Sure," I said. "The old Willie Wonder."

We reached the island, and watched the pelicans and cormorants scatter from the sandy beach. I began to troll around the lower end over a fairly shallow sandy bottom.

"There's an osprey nest up there," Hilde told me, pointing. "Up there on the highest cliff."

"I see it. There's a bird in it, too."

Then, the dorado hit hard. My reel screeched shrilly as the line went out. I cut the motor and turned to look, and 80 yards out the fish was in the air and then was gone, as quickly as that.

"Fifteen pounds," I said. "At least. You want to change to red-and-white?"

"No." Hilde looked determined now.

Ten minutes later, on the way back, farther out in deeper water, she hooked her fish.

This dorado didn't weigh 50 pounds—probably half that—but it did everything that Cannon had mentioned and more. It ran out at least half of her line—150 yards—from the strike. Once I cut the motor, the only sound was line hissing from the clickless saltwater reel. I watched the fish as it sped at a long angle away from the boat toward shore, its tail showing, with the monofilament leader cutting along, a surprisingly long way ahead of that tail. Then I turned to look at Hilde. She has caught a lot of good fish in rivers, lakes, and oceans, but with this one her face had gone pale, something I had never seen happen *anywhere*. "My God, it's strong!" she said. "I can't stop it. It won't stop."

"Let it go!"

I turned back toward the fish just in time to see it jump, and I silently prayed that the hook would hold. The fish, bright golden and blue in the sunlight, cleared the surface by at least 8 feet, and when he crashed back down and ran again, Hilde's rod remained bowed. He was well hooked. "You've got him!" I said.

Hilde did have him, but there were moments when she stopped believing it. Twice, the dorado—with well over 100 yards of line out—ran straight back at the boat, and the rod went dead for a minute or more.

"He's gone," Hilde said each time. "I think he got off!"

"Reel! Reel!"

Each time she reeled the line tight, the fish was there. He jumped often, sometimes several times in such quick succession that it looked as though three different fish were out there. He circled the boat. He sped beneath it. He cartwheeled. He thrashed. He ran again and again.

When Hilde finally had him up close to the boat—that critical time when many hooked fish are lost—her hands were shaking hard. She did a fine job anyway, and all the knots and the hook held. When I slid my hand down the leader toward the blue-and-white squid I could see that the hook was through the fish's upper lip.

"Don't kill him," Hilde said.

"What would two of us do with a fish like this?"

I thought I knew what would happen when I lifted the dorado from the water. "Take a good, close look," I told Hilde. Hook held hard in my right hand, I hoisted him up, all gold and blue and green—the most beautiful creature that lives on this planet, I believe.

With 2 feet of him out of the water, and nearly another 2 feet to go, he shook his large, blunt head, and the hook pulled out and he dropped back into the sea, as I thought and hoped he would. He barely made a splash, and disappeared so quickly that despite the clarity of the water, I couldn't tell in which direction he had gone.

"He's all right," I said. "He'll be fine."

"I did it!" Hilde answered. "I *did* it!" She literally screamed with happiness.

Fishing can make us young again, at least in spirit, and that is surely one of its principal virtues. Hilde's was the uninhibited and therefore perfectly lovely scream of a happy and healthy child.

Last Day   We thought of our last morning as a bonus. Whether or not we caught fish mattered little if at all. It was a chance to say goodbye to the area for a while, and to talk over what we had done and seen, and what we thought about it all, now that it was over.

No one was fishing the pier yet, so we trolled back and forth in front of it. By the time we came back in, that pier would be crowded with fishermen, most of them with handlines, a few with spinning or bait-casting rods, all of them using halfbeaks as live bait.

We had stood on the pier and watched the fishing several times, the Mexican men hauling dorado out of the water and ripping the hooks out, then tossing the fish onto the dirty, littered concrete. Within minutes the dorado had lost their color, and lay there coated with water, blood, and fine brown dust, amid plastic bottles and beer cans, pieces of discarded monofilament, and dried-up hunks of bait. The scene had disgusted me the first time I saw it. Now, though, I thought I understood. To Baja natives, fish have always been food. One look at the town of Loreto makes it obvious that meat fishing is still an economic necessity for these people. The fact that Hilde and I can fish primarily for sport doesn't mean we're superior, it only means we're lucky.

But we weren't lucky enough to hook anything in front of the pier, so we headed toward Danzante Island, straight into a brilliant orange sunrise. We trolled for four hours, with one break on the island where I'd hooked the seven dorado. There, on the sandy beach, we dug up some 6-inch cactus plants to take back home.

Halfway back to the bay, I caught a 3-pound dog snapper. "Should we keep it for lunch?" I asked Hilde, thinking of how the filets would look, striped from the hot iron grill.

"Let's eat fruit today," she said. "Rolando told me they'd have papaya at the store."

"So long," I said to the fish as I twisted the hook out. "It's been a perfect trip," I said to Hilde. "Should we come back in June?"

"I'd rather come when the weather's bad at home. Wouldn't you?"

"In a way. But there ought to be a lot of dorado here in June."

We argued about it—our first argument of the trip—the whole way in. Back in front of the pier again, which was crowded now, two dorado struck our bucktail flies. The red tips went down simultaneously. Hilde screamed, but only a little. Line peeled off both reels, but then Hilde's fish was gone, and a second later mine was.

"Too bad," Hilde said, smiling. "That would have been an exciting way to end it."

"It *was* an exciting way to end it," I said, reeling in. "Maybe they'll still be here when we come back next November."

Hilde's smile widened. "Maybe we ought to come in June."

Fishing from a Large Boat

The *Zucarita* is a very small boat by anybody's standards. What, though, is a large boat? For the sake of this discussion, a large boat is generally any craft 20 to 40 feet long or more, specifically meant for deep-sea angling. Such boats are equipped with bait tanks, fish boxes, fighting chairs, outriggers, a transom door for boating large fish, radios, and electronic depth finders (which locate fish as well as reefs, ledges, and drop-offs). For larger models, diesel motors are preferred over gasoline ones because of the increased range diesel fuel provides. The largest diesel boats are capable of covering hundreds of miles over a period of several days without returning to port. Smaller boats are designed for day trips of from six to twelve hours. Construction materials for these boats include fiberglass, wood, and metal, with glass most commonly used for smaller models.

To put these details into perspective, here are a few facts from the November 1984 issue of *Aquanotes,* a publication of the Center for Wetland Resources at Louisiana State University in Baton Rouge: There are 200,000 ocean fishermen in Louisiana, and the "typical" member of this large group is a thirty-five-year-old male with an income somewhat higher than the state average. Nearly three quarters of these men own boats, most of which are between 15 and 18 feet long, and which cost an average of $5,500.

If Louisiana fishermen are typical, this means that very few of us fish from large boats, unless it is from large boats that belong to somebody else. A well-equipped sport fisherman is a very expensive proposition, and it's doubtful that more than one saltwater angler in 10,000 owns his own boat. For 9,999 of us, there may be an occasional trip on a friend's boat, or a charter that we pay for.

As one of the 9,999, I have fished from large boats occasionally, mostly for marlin. When I recall these experiences I think of a fisherman named Guy de la Valdene, who wrote in *Gray's Sporting Journal* of "the immense boredom of off shore fishing."

It is necessary to mention this, because too few fishing writers give the matter the attention it deserves. It is unarguably true that deep-sea fishing can be and often is extremely boring. Though all of us have seen pictures and read accounts of leaping marlin and sailfish, few of us have read about the hours, even days, of waiting for such fish to be hooked. And the people who catch these large fish are understandably reluctant to acknowledge the fact that when the captain and the tackle are both first-rate, there usually isn't a great deal of skill involved in what they do. On any given day, an accountant from Cleveland has as good a chance of hooking a world-record fish as does an angler who has been out on the water thousands of times.

This, then, is the reservation many people have about going after big fish on large boats: long periods of inactivity are inevitable. For every dozen deep-sea trips taken, at least half, and possibly eight or ten of them, will very likely pass with little or no action. When action does come, there isn't much expertise required to handle it. Because of this, some of the excitement fades as soon as the novelty of large-boat fishing wears off. If you find hours or days of waiting tolerable, there's no problem. If you want fast action or a more sophisticated challenge, you will probably want to take up another form of the sport.

Obviously, though, there are tens of thousands of anglers who love deep-sea fishing from large boats, many of whom have no interest whatever in fishing any other way. What, then, are its appeals?

In a large, well-equipped boat it is possible, in relative comfort, to find what can justifiably be called the last true isolation on our planet. Out of sight of land, the world of sky and water is a genuine wilderness. Then add to this the fish that can be found there. To most anglers, a fish of 100 pounds is an enormous creature encountered only in dreams. In deep salt water, fish are caught that weigh 1000 pounds—and sometimes a great deal more.

Even if no great amount of skill is necessary to hook a large fish from a boat, there is usually some strength and courage required to land one. The fight can last hours, and can include painful aches in the legs, back, and shoulders, muscle cramps in the arms and hands, dehydration, severe headaches, dizziness, and nausea. I once read an account of a professional football player who, hooked to a big marlin, finally gave up on the fish, crying in pain.

Many experienced fishermen exercise in preparation for landing big game fish. They strengthen their arms, legs, and backs with exercises, and they crank reel handles thousands of times per day. On any except the very largest fish, it is the reeling muscles that are most apt to give you trouble. Unprepared arms and hands can become literally paralyzed with the seemingly simple effort of cranking a reel handle.

Not long ago I talked to a friend who had just returned from his first marlin fishing trip. "It's great when you first hook a fish," he told me. "The way they jump and run is fantastic. But when that's over with, it's just grunt work."

I know exactly what he means. A large game fish will almost always take out several hundred yards of line in the first few minutes after it is hooked. The drag setting on the reel has to be fairly light at this time. Inexperienced anglers tend to tighten their drags as fish take out line, when in fact the more line that a fish has out, the better off you are, assuming your reel has a sufficient capacity. It is the drag of line in the water that tires the fish, not the drag of reel. So, for the first few minutes after the bite, there is really little to do but sit, watch, and enjoy it.

But once such a fish has completed its initial run—and, most likely, its series of wild jumps—line must be regained by pumping the rod. The rod should be raised smoothly to take up some slack, then lowered as the reel handle is quickly cranked to claim that slack. With hundreds of yards of line out, this is a slow and tedious process. One pump of the rod may regain no more than a few inches of line, and never more than a few feet of it; it's not unusual for a good fish to make one long run after another over a period of several hours. This is when the captain of the boat, by careful maneuvering, contributes to the landing of the fish by regaining line with the boat.

Sometimes, just when you think you have won, a tiring fish will sound, and then your job is to lift it off the bottom, which is always a long way down. A captain is seldom of much help in this task, and the angler is apt to be very tired if not totally exhausted by the time this phase begins.

Several years ago in Hawaii, I happened to know a fairly young man who had become quite wealthy, thanks to an invention I never understood but which had something to do with jet engines. He used some of his money and most of his leisure time in pursuit of marlin in the deep waters of the Molokai Channel east of Oahu. I was primarily a spearfisherman and a light-tackle fisherman in those days, but he easily convinced me I ought to catch a large marlin with him. I think that what we experienced over a period of several days is a fair example of what marlin fishing is like.

We left the Honolulu docks at dawn each morning in a big boat of at least 40 feet, with two fighting chairs and 20-foot-long metal outriggers out each side at 45-degree angles to hold trolled baits outside the wake of the boat. "We'll fish two rods," my friend Tom explained. "A lot of people disagree with me, but I really think baits outside the wake draw more strikes. And a

59

lot of people around here think artificials draw more strikes, but I like fresh baits."

The heavy lines from the rod tips ran up to the tops of the outriggers, where they were clipped in place so that only the strike of a fish would release them. They were stiff, short, heavy glass rods, and the star drag reels held at least 1000 yards of line apiece.

"I've hooked big marlin right in here," Tom told me, "less than an hour out."

"How big?" I asked him.

"Four hundred and some pounds," he said, and I could see that simply mentioning such a weight made him excited. He was a former college football player, and he had stayed in shape. With his crewcut, dark tan, broad shoulders, and strong arms, he looked like a man who ought to be catching fish that size.

"What's the biggest one you've ever caught?" I asked him.

He smiled, his dark eyes shining. "A little over 700 pounds. Bigger ones are out here, though. Twice as big. *Three* times as big maybe. But nobody's caught one of those yet. Maybe you will. Do you know the rules? Once a fish hits, you're on your own. Nobody but you can handle the rod. Nobody can even *touch* it. A lot of records have been lost that way, especially on marlin."

"I know about that."

On the way out to the channel, Tom's excitement grew. "The most important thing," he said, "is to save your strength on a big fish. I realize you know how to fish. But with these big ones, even experienced people get pretty excited. I've seen them lose their heads. When that happens, they just waste their strength. Remember, in the beginning you can't do much and there's no sense trying. Once you get the hook set, for the next few minutes all you can do is hold on. The only time you can really tire a fish out is when it's swimming at a steady speed on a straight course. Then you just keep a heavy pressure on, and if I handle the boat right—and I will—it's the swimming that'll wear him out. You get tired pumping in line, he gets tired swimming. That's the key. Make him swim as much as you can and don't pump line unless it's doing some good. I'll get up on the flying bridge now. You stay back by the rods. Yell if you see a fish back there. If you get one following and he won't take, sometimes speeding up the boat draws a strike. I always say 'he' when I should say 'she.' Anytime you hook a big blue marlin, it's a female."

He climbed to the flying bridge and handled the wheel from there. I sat on one of the padded, comfortable fighting chairs and watched the baits that were 40 to 50 yards behind the boat. We were using flying fish of about 2 pounds, and I could see them clearly through the walls of the swells. One bait was a little farther back than the other, so I never saw both of them together. I imagined a huge marlin appearing behind one of the flying fish, taking it in its mouth, and turning with it. I watched hard for at least 20 minutes, but nothing happened.

We were well out by then—passing Waikiki Beach, a ribbon of white sand in front of a green wall of vegetation. We saw cumulus clouds over the mountain valleys, and a shower high in Manoa, with gray rain slanting into the steep, green slopes. Soon a rainbow appeared.

The boat rolled over good-sized swells with the motors running smoothly, almost too quiet to hear. Waves broke over the reef at Diamond Head. Then a school of bonito came out of the water near one of the baits. At first sight of the disturbance from the corner of my eye, my heart raced and I stiffened in the chair. Then, when I saw what it was, I thought that something big might have chased the bonito. I watched the baits, first one and then the other, whichever was visible, for several minutes. Nothing happened, though, and I relaxed again.

It was a relaxing day. The trade winds were pleasantly cool. Being on the sea is almost always nice, but out as far as we were, there wasn't much to see. The outlines of both Oahu and Molokai were purple-gray in the haze across the blue water. There were no whitecaps, but the swells, as usual, were fairly large. We saw a few other fishing boats, all of them a mile or more away. We saw planes on their way to and from the Honolulu airport. We saw cloud formations, gulls, flying fish, porpoises, and a school of tuna. We saw no marlin, though. We drank a couple of bottles of beer apiece, and we watched, waited, and then went back.

Tom wasn't particularly disappointed, and I wasn't, either. "Tomorrow," he said.

"Sure," I said. "Or the next day."

"That's the attitude," he said, smiling again. "Or the day after that."

So, the next day we went out again. On the way out, Tom put the lines in the water while I handled the wheel. He gave me some friendly advice. "It's easy to get discouraged along about the middle of the second day," he said. "You start to think marlin don't exist, at least not in these waters. But they do, and you want to stay ready for one. Sometimes they'll even pick up a bait and carry it a while and then drop it, and if you don't keep an eye on things you won't even know what happened or when. All of a sudden you notice the line's unclipped from the outrigger, and there's an extra two hundred yards off the reel. It's a lousy feeling."

"I believe it."

"I don't mean you have to stand next to the rods and stare at the baits all day."

"I know what you mean. Don't worry. I'll stay awake."

I did stay awake. For several hours, it was an exact repeat of the day before, except that we trolled a little closer to Molokai. That island was clearer, and Oahu was barely visible, through the haze.

It was minutes after we finished a lunch of cold sweet-and-sour chicken wings and beer that I made an awful mistake.

I saw the fish before it struck. I sat up stiff and straight in the chair, amazed, trying to convince myself that there really was a white wake on the blue water, a few feet behind the spot where I knew our portside bait had to be.

"Fish!" I screamed. "There's one there!"

Then, back beyond a smooth swell, a huge boil appeared on the water. Without knowing I'd left the chair, I had the rod in my hands. I saw the line pull free of the clip at the top of the outrigger, and, very quickly, the long loop of slack line hit the water and tightened. Line was running off my reel —dangerously fast it seemed to me—and I tightened the drag slightly with my right hand and dropped back into the chair, the butt of my rod in the socket. Then I struck the fish hard, four or five times, using all of my strength. For a few seconds I felt the great, unstoppable weight of the fish out there, surging away. Then, after one great thrashing on the surface 300 yards behind the boat, the weight was suddenly gone.

The calm that followed that moment was complete. I noticed that Tom had cut the engines to idling speed. "Too fast," I heard him say. "A little too fast. He was running with it in his mouth, just carrying it along." Tom sounded as disappointed as I felt. "Sometimes they hook themselves, right at the start, in the first instant. But sometimes they swim with it for a while, like that one did."

I was reeling in the line the marlin had run out. I felt drained and empty, almost sick, stupid, and guilty too. "I screwed up," I said.

"Not really. No matter how often you do it, it's hard to know exactly how to handle the strike."

"But I should have waited longer."

"A little. Just a little. Next time, why don't you let me tell you when to strike? I can see more from up here."

"Did you see the fish?"

"Sure, I saw him, after you yelled. Saw her. Twice. Once when she struck and then when she let go."

"How big?"

"Between three and four hundred pounds."

Tom rebaited with a fresh flying fish. The one that the marlin hit was mutilated. We trolled all day, but nothing else happened.

Nothing happened the next day either, except that the weather changed. The trade winds dropped off and the air became heavy and humid. Except for an irregular chop, the sea was calm. By noon I was sweating, even though I wasn't doing anything. "Kona weather" is what the natives call it. A spell can last for several days.

For some reason, my confidence died with the trade winds. By mid-afternoon of that third day I'd given up all attempts at staying alert. The sea seemed dead, with nothing showing on the surface. There weren't even any birds. It was an effort for me just to stay awake. Usually I'm mildly depressed at the end of any fishing day, because it's sad to have to quit. This time I felt relieved when we finally headed in, as the bow of the powerful boat cut through the chop, leaving a broad white wake behind us, the wind made by our speed cool on my skin.

The Kona weather held. It was very humid and already uncomfortably warm when we headed out the next morning. I asked Tom if weather like this had any effect on the fishing.

"It's like any other kind of fishing," he said. "If you talk to ten different people about it, you'll get at least six or eight different theories. All I'm sure of is that I've caught fish on days just like this one. If you do hook one, it'll be easier to play in water like this—easier for both of us."

No more than twenty minutes after the baits were out, the fish appeared. When I first saw it in the early-morning light, I didn't trust my eyes. The silver-gray flying fish was 60 yards back, just beneath the surface of the blue water, sometimes skipping across it. I remember that I was sitting on the fighting chair, leaning back comfortably, and daydreaming, when I noticed a long, slender form of slightly darker blue just a few feet behind the bait. It was moving steadily, effortlessly, and for several seconds I really did believe that what I saw was an optical illusion created by the movement of the boat, the dark water, and the early-morning light. I stood up and looked harder, and, once standing, I knew it was a fish. I yelled back at Tom: "Fish! It's following! It is one, isn't it?"

"Yes! My God! Look at her!"

I looked. The dark form stayed there, no more than a yard beneath the surface, neither moving closer to the bait nor dropping away.

Then, so quickly that I didn't see how it happened, the bait disappeared in a swirling splash of whitewater. I grabbed for the rod.

"Not yet!" Tom yelled. "He hit it with his bill!"

The bait was there again, skipping along, and I realized that Tom had increased our speed.

"Take the rod!" he yelled to me. "Get in the chair and get ready. But don't do anything until I tell you. I can see her pretty well from up here."

The fish followed for another half minute or more, without making another move at the bait.

"Free-spool the reel!" Tom yelled. "Put it on free spool and let the bait drop back!"

I did as he said. For ten or fifteen seconds I watched the water behind the boat as line spun from the reel, my thumb applying slight pressure to the spool. I couldn't see either the bait or the fish.

"She has it now!" Tom yelled. "Put the drag back on, and keep the rod up, but don't strike!"

As soon as I had engaged the drag, the line dropped free from the outrigger, and then I felt the weight of the fish. The tight line began to run out steadily and heavily. I leaned back in the chair, rod held high, the living weight of the fish moving steadily, unstoppably, away. The line was running off the reel a little faster all the time, and it seemed like a minute (though was probably less than half that) when Tom yelled again: "Tighten up just a little now and strike!"

I tightened the drag slightly and carefully, lowered the rod tip, then—putting my body into it—leaned back hard.

"Strike *hard!*" he yelled.

I did, several times. I felt the fish's weight out there, and, somehow, through all the line between us I could feel her beginning her first jump an instant before she came out of the water. I've never worked with dynamite, but this must be the feeling a person experiences when he presses the plunger down and waits for the blast—a blast that he knows is coming and to which he is directly connected, but that has a strength beyond his imagination.

The fish came all the way out of the water, writhing as it climbed, clearing the surface by several feet. It seemed to hang in the air, outlined against the dark blue water and lighter blue sky, its back an even darker blue than the water, belly silver, sides striped with vertical bars. Then it crashed back down, like a log smashing into the water, and I realized that Tom had the motors down to idling speed.

There were six jumps in the beginning, Tom counted them and told me later—and as I watched them, it was difficult to believe that I was attached to that fish, except for the living, heavy pressure on the bowed rod and the violent jolts of the line tearing from the big reel. With its last jump the marlin tail-walked straight away from the boat, churning the dark water white, and then ran several hundred yards so fast that I thought touching the line would have amputated a finger. Finally, the fish settled down and the work began.

It *was* work. I've played football and basketball in Hawaii, I've paddled in canoe races, and I've run the Honolulu Marathon through oppressive, humid heat. None of that compared with the physical effort that went into reeling in that fish.

I think I did a good job, and I know Tom did. He attached the harness around my back as soon as the fish settled down, reeled in the second line, and went quickly back to the wheel.

A fighting chair is designed to allow an angler to use his legs and back while pumping the rod to regain line. I was comfortable in the chair, and I took line whenever the marlin allowed it. But for the better part of three hours, when I gained 100 yards the fish would take back that much and more. She made seven or eight runs, and at the end of them all she had stripped more than half the line from the reel.

She was down fairly deep then, and swimming steadily, straight toward the island of Oahu. Tom kept the boat directly behind her, and I held on. After a while, Tom slowly angled up beside the fish, creating a belly of slack line which would drag between us, tiring her more quickly. The technique worked, because from that point on, whenever I gained 100 yards of line the fish would take back only 50 or 75.

But it tired me too. I felt the strain everywhere. My hands were nearly numb. I could barely open and close a fist. There were moments when I found myself hoping that the line would snap or the hook pull away. Of course I never said so. I said little through the whole fight, because talking seemed a waste of valuable energy. All Tom did was offer encouragement and occasional advice.

My memories of the last half hour of the fight are clouded by the fatigue I experienced. We were very lucky in one way, though. I remember how, because Tom explained it to me as it happened: "Lots of them sound at the end, and sometimes they die down there. Getting them back up can be an awful job. But I think ours is going to stay on top."

65

He was right, and toward the end, when we had her near the boat and on the surface, she jumped again, so close that cool water splashed against my chest and stomach. It felt good, and Tom laughed.

"Keep the rod up high," he said. "Just a little bit more. See the swivel? You can't reel past that. Okay! That's it! A little bit more!"

He had the wire leader in his gloved hand. I looked at the fish, wanting to remember it always—and I will. She was long, powerful, streamlined. She was on her side, showing shimmering, iridescent colors, a surprisingly blunt bill, long and graceful pectoral fins, and a huge, scythe-like tail. That tail was the source of much of her power.

I realized that I was standing up, looking over the transom at this beautiful fish. It was strange to be standing, and to suddenly have all strain gone from the rod, which felt weightless in my hands.

When Tom cut the leader the marlin righted itself at once, then sank slowly down and disappeared underneath the drifting boat. At that point I became aware of the absolute quiet.

"Congratulations!" Tom said, breaking the silence. "Pretty good fish! Better than 350 pounds!" He slapped me on the back, hard. Then he was shaking my hand with a powerful grip through a wet glove.

We fished two more days without a strike.

PART TWO

THE FISH

Presented here are descriptions of some widely sought saltwater game fish. The descriptions include physical characteristics of the fish, their habitats and distributions, and techniques, lures, and baits commonly used to catch them. My purpose is to give a representative cross-section of the hundreds of species of game fish available in salt water, so I've included different types and sizes of fish from various places. Some popular species have been omitted—jack cravelle, marlin, and dolphinfish, for example—because they are covered in other chapters of the book.

Following each description is a brief first-person narrative. These additional accounts of my own experiences are included because I think that example is at least as instructive as "how to" advice.

This material is meant to serve only as a beginning. As any reader, writer, or fisherman knows, local knowledge and personal experience are more valuable than even the most detailed printed advice. My hope is that what you find printed here will be incentive enough for you to seek out that experience.

Great Barracuda

Barracuda

Barracuda live in both the Atlantic and Pacific oceans, but the two species are very different.

The so-called great barracuda inhabits the Atlantic, from Florida southward to Brazil. It is a long, slim, silver fish with a large mouth and formidable teeth. Bars are visible on its back, and irregular black spots or blotches usually mark its streamlined body, most often near the tail. This fish reaches lengths in excess of 5 feet and weights of more than 50 pounds (the record is over 100). It is often said to be a danger to humans. If this is true, it is probably so only when an imprudent swimmer wears a silver wristwatch or sparkling jewelry, which might conceivably attract the strike of a feeding fish.

Though the real danger they pose to man isn't altogether clear, there is no doubt whatsoever that the great barracuda is a very aggressive creature. When a barracuda is feeding it will eat almost anything it comes across, which means that anglers can take them with surface plugs, baits, spoons, and flies. Strikes are often spectacular, especially on surface lures.

The kind of water you are fishing determines the kind of tackle that should be used. Large individual barracuda can sometimes be found in shallow water near shore, making either fly or light spinning gear worth a try. When casting, a rapid retrieve is often necessary, which can be tiring for a fly fisherman but worth the effort nevertheless. Most large barracuda are taken offshore on trolled bait.

The great barracuda is usually not considered a food fish, and in fact some of them are toxic, so there is little reason to kill one if you catch it. Therefore, rather than risk trying to remove a hook or lure from deep inside a mouth full of needle-sharp teeth, you may find it necessary to cut the line to let the fish go. Also, the use of wire leaders is a must.

Several species of barracuda inhabit the eastern Pacific Ocean, and the best known of these is the Pacific (or California) barracuda. Occasionally these fish are found as far north as Alaska, but are commonly caught from central California south to Mexico's Baja Peninsula. Any fish over 10 pounds is exceptional, and most are much smaller—from 1 to 3 pounds. Pacific barracuda, like their Atlantic cousins, are long and streamlined. They are dark-backed and silver-sided, with yellow tails and fins.

Fishing for Pacific barracuda in California is most productive during the spring and summer months, while farther south barracuda can be taken all year long. Unlike the Atlantic variety, Pacific fish are excellent to eat, though most experts agree that they should be eaten while very fresh. They can be caught by casting or trolling, and on both artificial and live baits. When casting, a fast retrieve usually draws the most strikes. Pacific barracuda often travel in huge schools, and on suitably light tackle they will provide excellent sport. Wire leaders aren't absolutely necessary, but if you don't use them you can expect to lose some tackle.

My most vivid memories of barracuda are of a large fish I caught off Marathon Key in Florida, and a whole school I found on a calm, hot afternoon in Baja.

Many years ago in Florida, a friend and I were fishing from an anchored skiff in about 30 feet of water, a few hundred yards off the lonely beach on which we were camped. We had light spinning gear—6-foot rods, 10-pound-test line, and silver spoons about 2 inches long. A school of bonito was feeding in the area, chasing baitfish across the surface all around our boat. They were 3-pound fish—no problem on our tackle—and we were catching and releasing them on nearly every cast.

Then, after an hour or more of this action, the bonito suddenly disappeared. We thought we saw some dark shadows near the surface 30 or 40 yards out from the boat, so we kept casting. After a few minutes my friend missed a strike from something that raced across the surface at great speed, leaving a wake behind it. As he reeled in to check his spoon, I cast as far as I could in the direction indicated by the wake.

I'll never know if it was the same fish, and it really doesn't matter, because almost as the spoon touched the water it was taken in a violent strike, and a barracuda that I judged to be 4 feet long jumped high from the water. The silver spoon was hanging from its mouth, shining as brightly as the fish in morning sunlight.

The fish crashed down and raced away.

We weren't using wire leaders, so it was something of a miracle that I stayed attached to that barracuda for more than an hour. It jumped several times and it made many long runs, taking out as much as 100 yards of line at a time. My friend rowed the skiff as I played the fish, and if he hadn't helped me recover line that way it might have taken all day to bring it up to the boat.

When we finally did manage to work the barracuda alongside us, we knew there was only one thing to do. The fish hung there in the clear water, its dark bars and spots and vicious mouth clearly visible. I took my pocket knife, reached over, and sliced through the monofilament near the waterline. The barracuda hesitated, but only for a moment. Then, almost too fast to see, it was gone.

The school of barracuda I found in Baja was as big a surprise as the single fish I hooked in Florida. It was a March afternoon, and I was fishing from rocks at low tide south of Nopolo Point, near Loreto. Sierra had been fairly thick in the area for almost a week, and I was casting white bucktail flies for them. Today, though, the sierra had disappeared.

After a couple of hours without a fish I came to a large, square rock that protruded farther into the water than anything around it. Because of the slow fishing, I had made my way farther south along the rocks than I'd ever been before.

When I climbed out as far as I could get and began to cast, it wasn't with a lot of hope. Then, on my very first retrieve, a 2-foot-long barracuda followed the fly almost to my feet. It didn't strike. The same thing happened for ten or a dozen casts in a row. I dropped the fly in deep water about 60 feet out from my rock, and from somewhere out there a barracuda would follow it in with its pointed snout inches from the fly. Then it would turn and streak away back to deep water whenever I had to lift the fly to make another cast.

I finally decided to speed up the retrieve, and it worked. The following barracuda came into sight about 30 feet out, and at that point I yanked in line as fast as I could. I never made more than three hard yanks before I had a strike. For 2 hours or more I hooked dozens of barracuda 2 to 3 feet long, and they gave me as much fun as anyone would want to have with a fly rod. I lost several flies, but the loss was more than worth it. Only the rising tide finally forced me to leave.

Bluefish

Bluefish

Bluefish are heavy-bodied, with blue-green backs, silver sides, and large, sharp teeth. Even though they are among the most popular of game fish, in an age of sophisticated biological research there are many unsolved mysteries regarding them. The most significant of these is why bluefish populations fluctuate so dramatically. During the season, for a period of several years, an area might contain hundreds of thousands or even millions of fish. Then, suddenly and for no discernible reason, these fish will suddenly disappear and stay away for years or even decades. At present the East Coast of the United States is experiencing a period of bluefish abundance which began in the late 1960s. Inevitably, this population too will disappear, but until that happens East Coast anglers will continue to enjoy some very productive fishing. (A relevant and fortunate footnote: Bluefish often are found in the same kinds of waters as striped bass, and have become abundant at the same time striper populations are rapidly declining.)

Bluefish occur in nearly all the warm seas of the world. In America they live from New England to Florida, with a few fish found farther north and south. South America, Africa, Spain, the Mediterranean, the Black Sea, the Indian Ocean, Australia, and New Zealand all have bluefish, and their maximum sizes vary according to location. Anywhere in America, a 10-pound fish is a good one, while in Africa bluefish are fairly commonly reported to reach weights of 40 pounds.

On our East Coast, bluefish usually begin to show in deep waters off Florida during the winter, and can be taken near shore by spring. By early summer fish are found as far north as New York, and soon after that in New England. In the fall they leave northern water, but can sometimes be caught all year off Florida.

One thing that bluefish everywhere have in common is their voracity. Many believe them to be the most ferocious fish in the oceans. They may even be a threat to humans. There are reports that schools of large bluefish attacked downed pilots off North Africa during World War II. There is no doubt that hundreds of careless fishermen have received painful and serious bites while handling and unhooking bluefish caught on hook and line.

Because they will attack virtually anything that moves through the water, and much that doesn't move, bluefish are often easy to see. Wildly-feeding schools will churn across the surface at full speed, with baitfish spraying in all directions ahead of them and birds wheeling and diving overhead.

They are caught from boats, and just as often from piers and beaches. When trolling, it is always a mistake to take a boat through the middle of a feeding school. If you troll around the edges, you will hook fish without disturbing the school. When casting for them, a fast retrieve usually works most effectively. Many anglers prefer metal lures, because a bluefish can chew anything else to bits before you land it. Wire leaders will save many lures and fish, but at times even bluefish can be selective and leader-shy, so it might be necessary to try several different lures and plugs and even to switch to monofilament. If fish should prove difficult to locate, chumming might work. Ground menhaden is often used as chum on the East Coast. When fish have been drawn to chum, live bait is usually more effective than dead.

As with catching most fish, suitable tackle is determined by weather conditions, the size of the fish, and the method of fishing. When a school of blues is encountered, every fish in it will be the same size, which is a distinct advantage in regard to choosing tackle. Some fishermen carry two or more outfits with them, including a fly rod.

I remember fishing for blues on a well-known East Coast beach. I won't name the place, because I didn't like what I saw there.

It was a humid fall afternoon, and I was with two friends. In truth, we went as much to cool off as we did for the fishing, which according to rumor hadn't been very good for several days. The wind was fairly calm, with a good surf rolling in. There were no more than half a dozen anglers spread over an area of at least 200 yards when we arrived.

We were casting metal plugs on 9-foot surf rods, and for half an hour or more nobody hooked a thing. Then, suddenly, everybody was hooking bluefish weighing about 8 pounds, and before long they were everywhere. They had forced bait in against the beach, in very shallow water.

We kept hooking good, strong, hard-fighting fish, one after another, and without my even realizing it, thousands of birds were overhead, diving into the bait schools. It was the birds that drew the fishermen, because not long after they arrived there were literally hundreds of people shoulder-to-shoulder along the beach, some of them standing back on dry sand, and most of them wading ankle- or knee-deep in the water, practically on top of the feeding fish.

I've never cared for mob fishing, or even for catching fish with every cast. You can't believe it until it happens a few times, but easy fishing quickly gets boring. Anyway, I quit, and before long my friends did too.

We stayed there and watched for an hour or more, and fishermen kept coming, parking their cars along the highway a couple of hundred yards back from the beach and running across the sand toward the water. They carried every kind of tackle imaginable, and not all of them knew how to use it very well. For every ten fish we saw hooked, I doubt that more than one was landed. There were fantastic tangles of line. Soon after the furor began, people were screaming and swearing at one another. There was at least one serious fist fight. Even though most fish broke off, soon there were hundreds of blues flopping on the sand.

The eager fishermen were still going at it when we left. I really don't know why we watched. It was probably because we'd never seen anything quite like it before. It wasn't a pleasant scene, though, and it's not my idea of fishing.

Bonefish

Bonefish

Bonefish grow almost as large as bluefish, to a maximum weight of about 20 pounds. Whereas bluefish often feed wildly and strike with utter abandon at almost anything (including each other), bonefish are among the most shy and difficult fish in the sea. They have bluish backs marked with dark bars over silver sides, and their colors often blend into the bottoms of the flats where they feed, making them very difficult to spot. Stalking them—seeing them before they see you—can be the most challenging aspect of the sport.

Bonefish can be caught on bait in deep water—in Hawaii, almost all of them are caught this way—but by far the most interesting bonefish fishing can be found in very shallow water, a few inches to 2 feet deep. The South Atlantic holds most of the world's best-known bonefish flats, and a majority of American anglers try for them in the Florida Keys. Like trout, bonefish that have been cast repeatedly become quite sophisticated, and in many areas, their acuity has made it much more difficult to hook them, some anglers say. Other anglers claim that bonefish have become used to boats and outboard motors, and that this has made fishing for them somewhat *easier* than it used to be.

Generally, bonefish move against a tide, or at angles to it. They feed by digging into the sea bottom for shellfish and mollusks, which they suck into mouths designed to grind hard food. Bonefish rarely, if ever, hold still. Sometimes a fisherman sees a tail out of water as a bonefish noses down to feed. Fish in deeper water are often spotted by the clouds of mud and debris they raise as they grub for food. If fish aren't tailing or digging, they must be sighted as they cruise steadily along just over the bottom. Small fish are apt to be found in schools, but (as with many species) larger fish tend to be solitary.

It is possible to wade a bonefish flat looking for fish, but most anglers, working in pairs or with a guide, travel in skiffs which are poled across the shallow water. Bonefish may be accustomed to boats, but the fact remains that dozens or even hundreds of them can be sent into a panic by a pole grinding clumsily against a coral clump, or by a single sloppy cast. When this happens, a flat that was covered with fish can be empty in seconds—empty, except for a fisherman or two who will most likely be feeling like fools.

Perhaps the easiest way to catch a bonefish is with a shrimp bait, which can be cast to sea as far as 20 to 30 yards ahead of a cruising fish and then left to sit on the bottom. Because the fish will be working its way into the tide, the smell of the bait is apt to attract him and draw a strike.

Next in degree of difficulty is a jig cast by a spinning rod. The success of this technique depends on the fish's sight, so the jig should be cast within a few feet of the target and worked in front of the fish with a slow, irregular retrieve. Some anglers combine jigs with strips of cut bait, such as bonito.

Sooner or later, most anglers who go after bonefish try a fly rod on them. A rather small bucktail pattern softly cast just ahead of a fish and retrieved with slow, foot-long pulls can produce some tense and exciting fishing. Sometimes a bonefish will follow a retrieve up to a boat or to an angler's feet before taking the fly (or, more likely, bolting away).

Writers sometimes slightly exaggerate the difficulty involved in fly fishing. It's not easy, but if you can cast softly and accurately for distances up to 50 feet, you can surely learn to hook bonefish. Ordinarily, the size of flies used depends on the size of the fish you expect to catch, and the weight of the fly is gauged by the depth of water in which you will fish. It has to sink near the bottom, but you don't want it to drag or snag. This method *can* become complicated, and has to be determined based on the size of the fish and depth of water.

Mornings and evenings are favored by most bonefishermen, because then winds tend to be calm and the water surface smooth, making casting easier and improving visibility. Wearing a good pair of polarized glasses is necessary at any time of day, and even with the best glasses bonefish can be difficult to see. Though as a general rule bonefish tend to move onto flats at high tide, many do not.

Light spinning or fly gear is preferred for bonefish, and using anything else is the easiest way to ruin the sport. Leaders of from 6- to 10-pound test are commonly used, and a quality reel with 150 yards of line is a must—or perhaps 200 to be sure. Bonefish don't strike hard, and don't jump, but once hooked they make straight, fast runs of 50 to 100 yards, often farther. There is a great contrast between the caution and delicacy often required to hook a bonefish, and the wild, powerful run that the hooked fish makes, leaving a wake across the surface as it speeds toward deep water. This sudden transition from forced calm to fast action is certainly one of the most exciting aspects of the sport.

I've caught many bonefish in Hawaii, but only on bait, and only with tackle that was much too heavy for them. A fishing companion once landed a bonefish of 17 pounds, which was nearly a world-record fish. But, because of the deep water we were fishing and the tackle we used, that fish did nothing spectacular, and was brought to the boat in 2 or 3 minutes.

Then, a few years later, I had a chance to try for bonefish in the Florida Keys. Because of my memories of Hawaii, I very nearly passed up the opportunity in favor of spearfishing. However, my friend insisted that catching bonefish in the Keys was very different, so with some reluctance I finally decided to go along.

I'm glad I did. He had an old wooden boat with a small and barely adequate outboard motor that we used to move us between the bonefish flats. We didn't fish from the boat, however, but anchored it and waded through water that was seldom more than knee-deep, searching for fish. We were using light spinning gear, 6-pound-test line, and lead-headed jigs.

For the first hour or so, all I did was follow my friend along and watch, which is as good a way as any to learn about a new kind of fishing. He explained the essentials of the sport to me, and I saw him cast to several fish and hook and land two of them, the largest between 4 and 5 pounds. A fish that size would have barely bent the rod I used in Hawaii, but my friend's little glass spinning rod was curved into a circle as the bonefish made that first hard run.

79

I made plenty of mistakes when I went off on my own. Wading quietly and slowly along in shorts and old tennis shoes, with the sun behind me, I was looking out ahead of me for fish to cast to when I nearly stepped on a small school of them and sent them rocketing across the surface toward deep water at least 100 yards away. A little later, I cast too close to a fish—in fact, I think I nearly hit it—and it disappeared in the same way. The first bonefish I actually hooked ran under a patch of floating seaweed, quickly snapping the line. The first and only fish I actually landed that day was an accident.

Because it was mid-day and the wind was up, making it difficult to spot fish from any distance, we stopped at a very shallow flat in from 6 inches to 1 foot of water. After half an hour of wading I spotted a good fish, its tail and a bit of its back showing, with mud and debris discoloring the water as it fed. I cast a few feet ahead of the fish and began a slow retrieve, but it ignored my jig and kept on feeding. So, when the jig was a safe distance away from the fish, I began to reel in quickly to try another cast. The fish that struck was no more than 15 feet away from me, and I hadn't even seen it. It weighed no more than 3 pounds, but catching it made for a very satisfactory beginning to a fine new sport.

Bonito

Bonito

Bonito simply aren't given the respect they deserve as game fish. Part of the reason for this is their relatively small size (anything weighing over 10 pounds is an exceptional fish). The fact that they are dark-fleshed and considered poor table fish—at least by Americans— is another reason for the low regard in which they are held. But bonefish don't grow any larger than bonito, and they aren't considered good eating either, yet anglers travel thousands of miles and spend great sums of money for a chance to catch one. From an angling viewpoint, the only real difference between the two species is that bonito are more widely distributed and far easier to catch than bonefish. While it may be human nature to value that which is rare more highly than that which is commonplace, it doesn't always make a lot of sense in fishing.

There are three subspecies of bonito, but their differences are meaningless to fishermen. These tuna-like members of the mackerel family all have blue backs marked with dark longitudinal stripes, and thick, powerful, bullet-shaped bodies. They can be found in rather shallow water and far out at sea, where they feed almost exclusively on schools of baitfish.

Like most fish on that diet, bonito will hit nearly anything that is trolled, and they can be taken easily on live bait. California fly fishermen have learned to appreciate bonito, and often the key to success with flies is a very rapid retrieve. Some experts make a long cast and then lay their rods in the boat, yanking in line as fast as they can with both hands to draw strikes.

No matter what a bonito hits, its strike is usually hard and its first run is deep, long, and powerful. Unlike many other game fish—including the bonefish—a bonito isn't tired out by its first run, and a 10-pounder on light tackle can keep an angler busy for half an hour or more.

The fact that bonito are fairly easy to find and will hit nearly anything should be appreciated. These fish can turn an otherwise dead day into a trip to remember.

Most of the bonito I've caught were hooked on trolled flies from small boats, but I've also caught some memorable fish from shore.

A few winters ago my wife and I were in Baja. We had fished from a boat from dawn until noon each day, trolling feathers for yellowtail, roosterfish, jack cravelle, and the occasional dorado. We also hooked and landed a number of good bonito, including a fish of 12 pounds caught by Hilde.

Then, after a few hours off, we fished the late afternoons and evenings from the rocky coastline a couple of miles south of our hotel. There we cast bucktail streamers on number-10 saltwater fly lines, and hooked barracuda, sierra, and ladyfish, none of them larger than 3 pounds.

It was pleasantly restful on a warm, quiet evening, watching the pelicans and frigatebirds as the sun set behind the steep black mountains, casting lazily, retrieving in steady pulls, the line stopping every 10 or 15 minutes and the rod suddenly bending into the solid resistance of a fish.

It was almost dark the evening I hooked my best bonito of the trip. In fact, it was well past the time most people believe it's possible to catch anything on flies. I have my own theory: When we look down into water on early mornings and late evenings, all we see is darkness, because we are looking away from the light. Fish, however, are looking out of darkness toward the light, and I'm convinced that they can see far better than we can.

Anyway, I was casting into the quickly-fading light, hoping for one last ladyfish. I had retrieved nearly all of my 60 feet or more of line, which lay in loose coils on the flat rock on which I stood.

The fish hit as if it was already traveling at full speed when it reached the fly. Bonito are said to be faster than any fish in the seas except for dolphin, wahoo, or billfish, and what happened to me that night proved that this must be true. My 60 feet of coiled line were gone before I could react. By the time I raised the rod the reel was already screeching. I was on a rocky point at least 200 yards from shore, and I know the bonito kept going at full speed until it was stopped by the beach itself. It was as long and as fast and as hard a run as any I've ever experienced from a fish of under 50 pounds. When I finally landed that fish, I honestly found it hard to believe that it weighed only 6 pounds.

There is no argument about it. Bonito are excellent fish.

California Yellowtail

California Yellowtail

The California yellowtail is a long, streamlined fish with a pointed snout, a blue-green back, greenish-yellow fins, and (of course) a yellow tail. One of the most popular game fish in the Pacific, it is found from the northwest well down into Mexican waters, but only in significant numbers from Southern California to Cabo San Lucas at the tip of the Baja Peninsula, and north into the Sea of Cortez as far as Bahia de Los Angeles. Concentrations of fish usually move north from Baja to Southern California in spring, and head south again during late summer and early fall, reaching the midriff section of Baja by November.

Yellowtails feed primarily on schools of smaller fish, and anything from sardines to small bonito or sierra make effective bait. At times they hit artificial lures or flies, which can be either cast or trolled. Though most yellowtails caught weigh less than 20 pounds, occasionally fish of 100 pounds are reported, and 30- to 40-pounders aren't uncommon. Even a 20-pound yellowtail is a very strong fish, and it can take a long time to haul one up out of deep water on light tackle—so long, in fact, that they can't be classified as light-tackle fish.

My experiences in Baja with yellowtails have been both confusing and enlightening. Following are some comments about these fish that I've heard over the years from various anglers.

"You can get them in shallow water right onshore early in the mornings. They drive the baitfish in, and when they do that you can catch one on a bare hook."

"You have to fish down deep for yellowtails. Live bait on the bottom in deep water is the only thing that works."

"The only thing I've ever caught yellowtails on is big lures. I anchor at the mouths of small bays and cast toward shore from there."

"The best yellowtail fishing is in November and December, right after they get here."

"The best yellowtail fishing is in March, right before the fish leave."

All of these remarks came from experienced and skillful fishermen, and I'm sure that, at some times and in some places, all of them are true. The only reasonable conclusion to draw is that yellowtails are not nearly as predictable as most fishermen would like to think they are.

On a family vacation in Baja one spring, my wife and son and I were trolling for sierra and jack cravelle. We weren't interested in yellowtails, because even though there were good numbers of them in the Loreto-Mulege area, word was out that they were holding near the bottom in deep water. The standard fishing procedure in this case would have been to motor far offshore and either anchor or drift with live bait several hundred feet down. On a good day, six hours of such fishing will produce a fish or two per rod.

We much preferred to take our chances near shore, and for several days we had good if not spectacular fishing. The jack cravelle were particularly thick. Meanwhile, the hotel guides came in at noon each day empty-handed, with two or three glum-looking clients per boat.

At dinner the evening before our last day of fishing, I got into a conversation with two young men at the next table.

"We've been here three days and haven't caught a yellowtail yet," one of them said.

"It's the most boring damn fishing trip I've ever been on," put in the other. "Sitting out there bobbing around for half a day and watching the sky isn't too exciting. Tomorrow we're going to talk the guide into trolling near shore."

"He's refused to even try it so far," said the first young man. "He keeps saying, 'It won't work.' But what the hell, what we're doing now sure isn't working. Maybe he just wants to save gas."

The next morning Hilde stayed at the hotel and my son Pete and I went out fishing. It began as our slowest day of the trip. We trolled south along the coast for several miles without a strike. We trolled back the way we'd come and picked up two or three small fish. Finally, Pete tied on a large feather lure and immediately hooked a yellowtail. Then I hooked a dorado. Then Pete hooked another yellowtail. Unfortunately, the wind came up and we had to head in.

When we saw the two young men at lunch, one of them told us: "At first we couldn't get the guide to troll. He just kept shaking his head and saying it wouldn't work. So we sat out there for about four hours and didn't hook a damn thing. Finally we talked him into taking us back toward shore. We used our Spanish dictionary. We told him we didn't care if we caught any fish, we just wanted to move around for a change. We pleaded with him, and he finally shrugged his shoulders and smiled at us like we were idiots, but he started in. Well, as soon as we got inside Carmen Island we tied on lures and started trolling, and those lures weren't thirty feet behind the boat when we both hooked yellowtails. It was fairly shallow water, forty feet or so, and we kept hooking yellowtails until the wind came up. We got six apiece."

The next morning, before we left for the airport, I scanned the sea with my binoculars. Dozens of boats were out there trolling for yellowtails, and undoubtedly catching them. My only real regret was that we hadn't tried casting for them from shore.

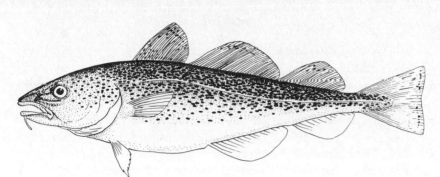

Cod

Cod

Atlantic and Pacific cod are similar, though cod are most commonly sought as game fish in the Atlantic Ocean. Cod are built much like trout, though somewhat heavier, and their colors range from red to gray and sometimes include shades of green and brown. They are large-mouthed cold-water fish most common in the Atlantic from New England northward, though they are found as far south as the Carolinas. Their pattern of distribution is similar out West, where cod occur most abundantly from Oregon northward, though they can be found as far south as central California. Small cod usually swim close to shore, while large fish inhabit deep water of up to several hundred feet. Most cod caught weigh less than 10 pounds, but fish of more than 100 pounds are taken now and then. Effective cod baits include strips of fish, small whole baitfish, and clams. Jigs are sometimes useful, and it is possible to take cod trolling lures which resemble baitfish, if the lures are heavily weighted and trolled near the water's bottom. Most cod are caught still-fishing in fairly deep water, with stiff rods and strong saltwater reels (not spinning reels). Half-pound sinkers are frequently needed, so light tackle is very rarely useful.

When I lived in New England for a year, I went out after cod on party boats several times in mid-winter. It was always cold and almost always windy.

We fished in 200 to 300 feet of water, sometimes anchored, sometimes drifting. It always seemed to me that drifting worked best, but often it was too stormy to do so. There wasn't anything delicate about the fishing. We used surf-casting tackle and clams for bait. There were twelve or fifteen of us on a boat, and on good days at least one person had a fish hooked all the time. We fished the clams on the bottom, and the cod usually hit hard, hooking themselves suddenly. The biggest fish I ever caught weighed just over 40 pounds, but I saw some taken that weighed over 60 pounds. Cod are strong fish, but not spectacular. They make short, hard runs as you work them up, and it can take quite a while to wear out a big one—even when using 40-pound-test line, as we were.

I liked the companionship on those boats as much as I liked the fishing. We were wearing about five layers of clothing each, and we talked and joked as we fished. My hands were constantly numb despite heavy gloves, my nose was always running, and my feet were so senseless that for half an hour after we got back to port it was difficult to walk. Maybe cod are a masochist's fish. In any case, when fishing in cold weather people seem friendlier to one another, and it must be the mutual suffering that makes this so.

King Mackerel

King Mackerel

These are the largest of the American Spanish mackerels, commonly reaching weights of 20 pounds and sometimes more than 80 pounds. They are slim, strong, sharp-toothed fish, and, except for the largest individual mackerel, they usually travel in huge schools which follow a fairly predictable seasonal migration pattern up and down the Atlantic Coast. As with bluefish, their populations fluctuate between great abundance and relative scarcity over the years.

Though king mackerel can be found as far north as New England, most serious fishing for them takes place along the coasts of Florida and the Gulf of Mexico during the cool months. Spinning tackle with line of up to 40-pound test and wire leaders are used to catch them, although revolving spool reels are preferred by some, particularly for drift-fishing. Jigs, plugs, sub-surface lures, flies, live bait, and strip bait are used with success, and the choice among them depends upon your personal preference and whether you are trolling, casting, or drift-fishing. King mackerel can be chummed to the surface, where you can try for them with surface plugs or streamer flies.

A trip I took on a charter boat off the Gulf Coast of Texas was a fairly typical one for king mackerel fishing. We were trolling jigs on medium-weight spinning gear, and our guide had explained that we were looking for school fish in the 10-to-20-pound range.

We looked for a couple of hours without success. Finally, we got into a good school. When we did, the guide cut the motor and we fished by drifting strips of cut bait from the first king mackerels we caught, which we weighted with small sinkers. These fish hit the cut bait very hard, and their first long runs were extremely powerful. Sometimes king mackerel jump, but none of the ones we hooked that day did. In fact, we never saw them on or near the surface. Whenever we went several minutes without a strike, the guide maneuvered the boat until we were above the school, and then the action resumed.

Before long, several other boats had joined us, both charter boats and private ones. The day was cloudy, but warm and humid, and the sea lay calm to the horizon. Sound carries well over water, and we could hear the conversation from other boats around us as anglers of various temperaments and degrees of skill worked their king mackerel in. There were thirty-five or forty fishermen there in eight or nine boats, and at times nearly every one of their rods was bowed, the monofilament lines slanting at various angles into the dark water. Laughter, excited talk, and occasional mild profanity filled the air. Landed fish could be heard thumping hard against the decks of the boats.

The three rods on our boat accounted for the catch of at least forty king mackerel weighing up to 15 pounds, and between all the boats in our little group hundreds of fish must have been landed. After about an hour and a half we lost the school, and the action ended as quickly as it had begun.

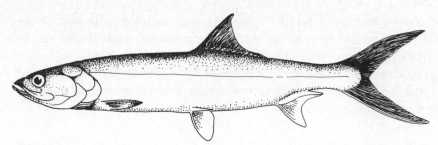

Ladyfish

Ladyfish

The ladyfish, found in the Atlantic, Pacific, and Indian oceans, is perhaps the smallest legitimate saltwater game fish. Ladyfish weighing more than 5 pounds are considered trophies, and most weigh half that much, or less. Yet, on very light tackle, they can produce real excitement.

This is a lovely fish: long, slender, finely scaled, of bright silver with a blue-green back. It is commonly caught in the warm waters of Florida, the Gulf Coast, and the Carribean. In the warmest waters of the Pacific, it is also abundant.

A cousin of the tarpon (about which more will be said later), the ladyfish is a wild jumper. Large schools of them travel and feed together, and are usually encountered in fairly shallow water close to shore. Sometimes they prefer brackish water, or water clouded by sand. They also seem particularly easy to catch after the sun has set. It's not unusual to fish an area for a couple of hours without any sign of ladyfish, and then to hook one after another just before darkness sets in.

Baits, jigs, spoons, plugs, and flies will all take ladyfish, and the key to your enjoyment is to catch them on the lightest possible tackle. A light wire leader is sometimes useful, but not because of the ladyfish's teeth. Its scales are very abrasive and can wear through monofilament as quickly as sandpaper. A tippet of heavy monofilament—20-pound-test—will usually last through several fish if no wire is available. In this case, the tippet should be checked after each fish is landed. When the abrasion has become severe, a few inches of worn leader can be clipped away and the hook, lure, or fly retied. Whatever lure is used to catch them should be retrieved rapidly. Ladyfish are very bony, so there is little sense in killing one unless there is an urgent need for a meal.

My most interesting day with ladyfish occured on the Sea of Cortez in the fall of 1984.

Hilde and I were trolling streamer flies in 10 or 12 feet of water about 50 yards out from a sandy beach. We were hoping for jack cravelle, and when the first hard strikes came—a double hook-up—that was what I thought we had found. But instead of starting the long, hard run of the jack, these fish immediately leapt high out of the water, shining as silver as coins as they twisted and writhed in the sunlight. We knew at once that we had found a school of ladyfish.

After we landed that first pair, we switched to the light fly rods we often carry for just such times. They were trout rods that we normally use for stream fishing in Oregon, with simple single-action reels, weight-forward fly lines, and white-and-yellow streamer flies.

We trolled back and forth along that beach for an hour or more, hooking two fish at a time every couple of minutes. Sometimes a fish came off before we had it in the boat, but whenever that happened another ladyfish would strike within seconds, on the first or second yank of the fly through the water. The area was thick with them. Whenever I stood in the boat I could see hundreds of fish all around us, moving in undulating waves just beneath the surface.

Finally we stopped the boat and let it drift to cast for them, which proved even more effective than trolling. The only reason we quit was that we finally grew tired of landing and releasing fish.

"It's just too easy," I said to Hilde.

As I said that, I realized that back home I often cast all day long for a single steelhead, and that few steelhead jumped or fought as well as these fish did. Such is the life of an angler.

About an hour later, when we were almost back in Escondido Bay, we ran into another huge concentration of ladyfish, and we stopped to cast for them. These fish were schooled in about 10 feet of very clear water near a mangrove bank, and I was sure it was going to be more of the same kind of fishing.

"We might as well hook ten or twenty before we head on in," I said to Hilde.

So we began to cast, but we didn't catch ten or twenty. We didn't catch a single one. When we dropped our flies a few yards away from the school, the fish paid no attention to them. When we dropped our flies even closer, the fish scattered in wild panic. I tried casting from farther away, with the sun behind the boat. We tried different colors and sizes of flies, and different speeds of retrieves. We worked at it for an hour or more, trying everything we could dream up, and we never had so much as a half-hearted strike for our trouble.

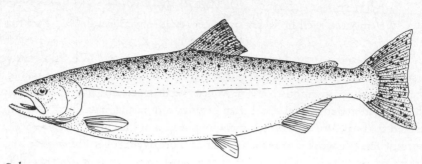

Salmon

Pacific Salmon

Of the five North American species of Pacific salmon—sockeye, pink, chum, chinook (often called king), and coho (often called silver)—only the chinook and the coho are important saltwater game fish.

The chinook is the larger of the two species, commonly reaching weights in excess of 30 pounds and averaging about 20 pounds. Occasionally, fish of more than 100 pounds are taken, usually in Alaskan waters. Coho average less than 10 pounds, but despite this they are considered by many anglers to offer better sport than chinook. This is because coho can often be caught at or near the surface, on light fly or spinning gear, by either casting or trolling. When hooked, they are wild jumpers and fighters. Chinook are almost always down 100 feet or more, and heavy gear is necessary to reach them. They usually fight, too, even down deep.

Pacific salmon ascend their parent streams to spawn, and fishing for them is possible when they gather outside the mouths of their rivers prior to spawning runs. Most chinook enter fresh water in the spring or fall, though there are rivers here and there which attract fish nearly all year long. Most coho runs are in the fall. Salmon stop feeding as soon as they enter fresh water, so they gorge themselves until that time, building up reserves of energy to carry them upstream against powerful currents, sometimes for hundreds of miles.

Both coho and chinook are most often caught by trolling with herring, though some fishermen prefer large silver spoons. Whole herring or strip baits can be used, and in either case trolling speed should be fairly slow. There are many ways to rig baits so that they either spin or undulate when drawn through the water. A fisherman can learn the most effective rig for any area at a local tackle shop, or by asking a resident. Twelve-pound-test line is adequate for catching coho, and 20-pound-test is usually considered a minimum for chinook.

The most productive areas for offshore salmon fishing are easy to find. From central California to Alaska, dozens, sometimes hundreds, of commercial, charter, and private boats will crowd favored spots from morning until night throughout the season.

Despite these crowds, there is still some good fishing available. Sadly, salmon runs have decreased markedly throughout this century, and particularly in the last twenty years. Commercial fishermen are taking too much of the salmon population. One river after another has been dammed. (The Columbia, once North America's greatest salmon river, is now little more than a series of reservoirs.) Pollution has been a major damage factor, as has logging, which removes shade, and thus raises water temperatures, and causes siltation of gravel spawning beds.

Once a friend and I lucked into some coho fishing off the mouth of a rather small Oregon coastal stream. It was early in the season—maybe too early, we thought—and we were trolling a couple of hundred yards out from a concrete pier where half a dozen bait fishermen were sitting on lawn chairs watching their rods and waiting for something to happen.

It was a warm morning, just at the change of tide from high to low, and we suddenly found ourselves in a school of feeding coho. The sea was calm enough and clear enough for us to see the salmon chasing after baitfish, and our only problem was the speed with which they were moving. We had a small boat and motor, and it wasn't always easy to get ahead of the feeding fish and then swerve around them, dragging our silver spoons across their path.

But whenever we did get a lure in front of them we hooked fish, usually two at a time. They weren't large—only 5- and 6-pounders—but, once hooked, they spent nearly as much time in the air as in the water.

Our hot fishing lasted only about an hour. By then, twenty-five or thirty other boats had joined us. The fishermen on the pier must have seen us landing fish and spread the word, and the rapid result was this aquatic traffic jam. There are seldom any secrets in salmon fishing.

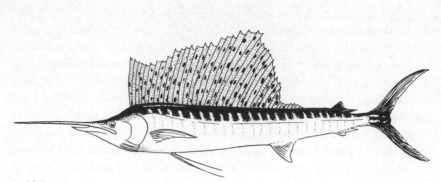

Sailfish

Sailfish

Some anglers are of the firm opinion that sailfish are more fun to go after than marlin, citing three reasons. First, sailfish are more numerous and therefore easier to find than marlin. Secondly, they are big enough to generate as much excitement as the best fish, but not so big that it takes hours to land them. Finally, sailfish have proved to be quite catchable on light tackle, including the fly rod.

In the Atlantic, sailfish weigh an average of less than 50 pounds, with a few topping 100 pounds. For reasons no one understands, Pacific sailfish are more than twice as large as their Atlantic counterparts. Except for this difference in size, the fish are identical, with dark blue backs, silver sides marked with pale vertical bars, and white bellies. The rear half of their purple dorsal fin, or sail, is covered with small black dots. Like dolphinfish, sailfish can change colors when they become excited, and no angler who has seen this happen will ever forget it.

Most sailfish are caught by trolling either strip bait or whole dead bait at a speed which causes it to skip across the water. Live bait is trolled beneath the surface at somewhat slower speeds, about 5 to 7 miles per hour. Revolving spool reels, wire leaders, and line in the 20-to-40-pound-test range are ordinarily used. Like marlin, sailfish will very often follow a trolled bait a long way before taking it (or, more likely, turning away from it). Sometimes slowing or even stopping the boat will draw a strike at this point. When a sailfish does strike, the standard procedure is to throw the reel into free spool, wait between 5 and 10 seconds, then brake the reel and set the hook.

Casting for sailfish has become quite popular in recent years. The common technique is to troll a bait or teaser without a hook, and when a sailfish appears, to pull the bait or teaser slowly toward the boat until the sailfish following has been lured within casting range. Sailfish of more than 100 pounds have been taken by fly fishermen on 12-pound-test leader tippets. Any streamer fly seems to work. Plugs and lures are also effective.

An experienced angler can usually land a 50-pound sailfish on a 12-pound-test tippet in half an hour to forty-five minutes. Because they aren't good table fish, most sailfish are released. However, landing and releasing them can be tricky, because their bill is a formidable weapon. A sailfish should never be gaffed and dragged into a boat and allowed to flop wildly around. It can be pulled in by the bill, but in this case wearing gloves is definitely necessary. If the fish is to be released, the simplest way to do so is to cut the leader near the fish's mouth without taking the fish out of the water. Salt water will soon dissolve the hook.

I was fourteen years old when I saw my first sailfish. I was in Hawaii, off Molokai, and I had been invited trolling by two Hawaiian fishermen. We used a boat that was an interesting combination of the old and the new—a koa wood canoe, with an outboard motor clamped to the rear outrigger.

We were trolling dead mullet on two rods, which were held by Dad, who was handling the motor, and by Jerry, a younger man who had the seat ahead of him. I was in the passenger seat up front. We had been out two or three hours without a strike when the sailfish appeared.

"My God!" said Dad. "Look at that! He's hitting it with his bill! Take it! Take it!"

The fish did take it, just as I turned in my seat to watch. I'd never seen anything quite like what happened then. No more than 50 feet behind the canoe, the sailfish came up out of the water, its barred blue-and-silver body curved nearly into a circle at the top of its leap. It crashed down and ran, and then, 75 or 100 yards out, it jumped again and again.

At this point, Jerry handed me the rod. "See if you can bring him in," he said, laughing.

I brought him in all right—it took half an hour, they told me later, though it seemed more like five minutes to me—and during the entire time I don't think the fish stopped moving. If I wasn't pumping the rod to regain line as quickly as I could reel, I was watching it disappear from the reel as the sailfish ran. He stayed on or near the surface from beginning to end, jumping often, and when I finally did bring him up near the canoe we could see all his gorgeous colors—purple, blue, silver, black—in the sunlight through the clear water. He was 8 or 9 feet long.

Dad reached down quickly with a knife and cut the leader. The sailfish hung there for a few seconds, then eased away and down. I had never felt a fish like that at the end of a line before, and I'd never seen anything quite so lovely. We caught some other fish that day, but I don't remember what they were. It would have taken a whale to impress me after that experience.

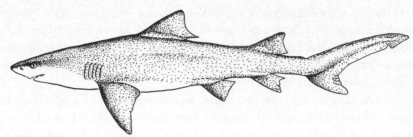

Lemon Shark

Sharks

Thousands of anglers have taken up shark fishing in recent years, for many good reasons. Sharks exist in large numbers nearly everywhere. Several species—makos, threshers, blues, blacktips, bonito sharks, sand sharks, tiger sharks, and others—have gained deserved reputations as strong and sometimes spectacular fighters. Nearly all of the sharks that can be taken on rod and reel fight decently when hooked, and some of these species grow to extremely large sizes. 1000-pound sharks aren't uncommon, and great whites of more than 3000 pounds have been taken by sportsmen. Americans are learning that many sharks provide good-to-excellent eating. On the East Coast, bonito sharks and threshers are among the most highly regarded for food, while blues and makos are often sold as swordfish in the West, because their taste is indistinguishable.

Most sport fishing for sharks is done with bait, and sharks are usually attracted to a boat—or occasionally to shore—by chumming. Nearly anything that happens to be available can be used as chum, with chopped baitfish or squid most commonly used. Ground menhaden is widely used on the East Coast.

The most productive areas for chumming from off a boat are where schools of the fish that sharks normally feed on can be found. If bonito or mackerel are showing, it's a near certainty that sharks are nearby. When sharks do show on the surface, they can be hooked on strip bait or whole bait, either slowly trolled or drifted. Most anglers who drift their baits use cork floats to keep them near the surface with the chum. After taking a bait, a shark will often carry it a considerable distance before swallowing it, so it is a rule of thumb to wait 30 seconds or a minute before setting the hook.

Some sharks, such as the mako and thresher, will leap from the water several times after feeling the hook. Most sharks will make long, powerful runs. The tackle to be used for sharks depends on the species and size of shark sought, but wire leaders are always advisable. For anyone planning to go after sharks for the first time, it is definitely a good idea to bring along someone with experience.

Help and expert advice are most important when it comes to boating a shark. It is a large, powerful, aggressive creature, and gaffing one that has not been played out can be a disaster. Even bringing a green shark close to a boat for release can be dangerous. This fish has been known to rip large chunks from wooden hulls.

Some species of sharks are commonly encountered by light-tackle anglers fishing from shore. These shallow-water sharks include the blacktip, sand shark, and lemon shark. Specimens as large as 100 pounds are occasionally found near the beach, and when there, they sometimes hit plugs or flies. The standard shark-fishing technique is to cast directly in front of the target, and then retrieve slowly. Sharks have poor eyesight, and a lure dropped just a few feet away from one, or yanked quickly away, will most likely be ignored.

My own shark fishing has always been interesting and instructive, if not always altogether enjoyable.

When I was in high school, a friend of mine and his father took me with them to a rocky point near Oahu's north shore. There we met with three other men who had arrived ahead of us with a truckload of waste from a slaughterhouse. This waste included animal parts, entrails, and bloody skins. Hundreds of pounds of this chum was tossed off the point into the deep water, where it floated, or very slowly sank, and spread.

Within a matter of minutes sharks appeared. Four or five dorsal fins were cruising back and forth, no more than 20 yards from where we stood. Soon there were fifteen or twenty of them. We couldn't see them clearly enough to determine their species, but we began to cast.

We had surf-casting outfits, with whole small tuna for bait, and we hooked several of the sharks, but we didn't even come close to landing any. Each time one of us had a hooked shark under control, other sharks attacked it, and within a minute or two had torn it apart. Either the teeth of the attacking sharks or their abrasive skins cut our lines in the process, and after this had happened several times we gave up.

For a long time we stood there watching. The sea was red with blood, and sharks kept arriving to join in the increasingly savage feeding. It was one of the most impressive and frightening sights I've ever seen in the sea.

A far more satisfactory angling experience occurred one bright, hot July day on the Sea of Cortez. I was walking down a sandy beach after a long morning's fishing, heading back to my hotel. The day was calm, and out of the corner of my eye I caught a movement on the smooth surface of the water.

When I looked I saw a dorsal fin cutting along about 30 yards out. I could see the shark too, about 4 feet long, swimming at a slightly faster pace than I was walking, in the same direction.

I jogged down the beach to get well ahead of the shark, then waded out to knee depth and false-cast line until I had as much in the air as I needed. Then I dropped my red-and-white streamer fly a couple of feet ahead of the shark's blunt nose. I retrieved the streamer in foot-long pulls as the shark swam by, but he made no sign that he cared about the fly, or even that he saw it.

I repeated this maneuver six or seven times—jogging ahead, wading in, casting the streamer, and pulling it back. Finally, on a cast that was exactly like all the others, the shark grabbed the fly a second after it touched the water, and I set the hook hard.

About an hour later, after many strong runs and a dogged fight, I had a lemon shark at least 4 feet long close enough to cut the leader.

It was far from the most spectacular fish I've ever caught, but it was certainly more than I'd bargained for that morning.

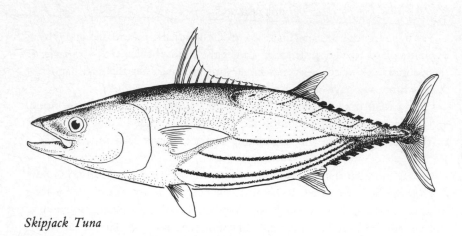

Skipjack Tuna

Skipjack Tuna

The skipjack tuna goes by many names, including striped tuna, little tuna, and oceanic skipjack. It is another member of the mackerel family, streamlined and powerfully built, with longitudinal black stripes on its silver belly. It looks like a bonito, except that a bonito is striped on the *upper* half of its body. Skipjacks reach lengths of 3 feet and weights in excess of 30 pounds, but 8 or 10 pounds is closer to an average weight. The species is found in warm seas everywhere, and sometimes travels in schools of several thousand fish. It is an important commercial fish in the Pacific, and an important game fish, too. It can often be found closer to shore than other tunas, and can be caught by casting, trolling, or still-fishing. It strikes many varieties of baits, plugs, and lures, and will also hit streamer flies.

One day when I was out with Tom the marlin fisherman (see "Fishing from a Large Boat"), we ran into a large school of skipjacks. He cut the motor, and we drifted over them for an hour, casting plugs on the lightest rods he had aboard. The fish struck hard, and, once hooked, made long, deep runs. We landed dozens of them, and released all except for some 4- and 5-pounders that Tom wanted to keep for baits.

As we cast, reeled, hooked fish, played them, and landed them, our conversation turned to tuna fishing in general. Tom had caught all species, including Atlantic bluefins, which reach weights of more than 1000 pounds.

I had already landed my marlin, and I thought the bluefins sounded intriguing. "I'd like to try for one sometime," I said.

"Don't bother," Tom said. "That's my advice."

"Why not?"

"Because they're even more work than marlin. They're *all* work. You get a good hard strike—sometimes you do—and then one long run, and when that's over all you do is break your back for a few hours. They're as big as marlin, and if anything even stronger, and they don't waste their energy jumping. A big bluefin can tow a good-sized boat for miles. They didn't even have tackle that could handle them until the 1930s. I love to fish as much as anybody, but I've had enough of bluefins to last me the rest of my life." He hooked another skipjack and smiled. "As far as tuna are concerned, I'll take these or yellowfins anytime."

"I'd still like to try it," I said.

I haven't hooked a bluefin tuna yet, but someday I hope to—at least one. Meanwhile, I'm still enjoying skipjacks every chance I get.

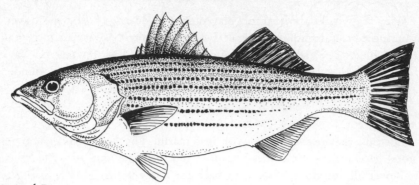

Striped Bass

Striped Bass

Striped bass populations on both coasts have declined drastically in recent years—some experts estimate as much as 90 percent in a few locations. Though there are commercial interests and politicians who find it advantageous to debate the issue, the reasons for this decline are clear.

On the East Coast, acid rain is mostly to blame. Stated simply, the problem is that striped bass cannot spawn successfully in acidic water, which is what the smokestacks of our industries are giving them these days, particularly in the vast and crucial habitat of Chesapeake Bay. This problem has become so severe that the state of Maryland banned both commercial and sport fishing for striped bass beginning January 1, 1985. Out West, the problem is that the spawning waters in the bays and deltas of central California are being diverted south for various commercial uses, raising the salinity of the remaining water to a point that makes spawning almost impossible. If things continue as they have been, some environmentalists fear, the striped bass will virtually disappear. If this ever happens, we will be losing a resource of immense value.

Striped bass are powerful fish with dark backs, silver sides, and longitudinal black stripes. They are very active feeders, and can be caught from beaches or from boats seldom more than a few miles offshore by trolling or casting. Fish of more than 100 pounds have been recorded, but anything weighing over 30 pounds is considered large these days.

On the East Coast, "stripers" can be found from Canada all the way to Florida and across the Gulf of Mexico, with the best fishing found from Massachusetts to the Carolinas. The season, with local variations, runs from spring through fall, with the largest fish taken in the warmest months.

Striped bass aren't native to the Pacific Coast, but were introduced into San Francisco Bay in 1886 in one of the most fortunate fish-planting experiments ever conducted. The Bay Area continues to provide the best striper fishing, with its peak during the summer. In fall these fish migrate into the deltas and remain there during the winter to spawn in the spring. Stripers are caught in decent numbers as far south as the Monterey Bay area, and sometimes all the way to Los Angeles, especially during recent years. Good northern areas include the Coos Bay and the Columbia and Umpqua River areas of Oregon. While Atlantic stripers will usually hit spoons, plugs, squids, blood-worms, and flies, Pacific fish sometimes prefer anchovies, though they are taken regularly on lures and flies.

On either coast, the tackle used for catching striped bass is determined by where and how you are going to fish for them. A good all-around bass-fishing outfit might include a strong eight-foot spinning rod with a well-made reel holding a couple of hundred yards of 15-pound-test line, and a good collection of plugs, lures, sinkers, hooks, and baits. This outfit would catch fish either from shore or from a boat, under most conditions. However, where extremely long casts are necessary, a surf-casting rod would be a better equipment choice.

When I lived in San Francisco, back in the days when stripers were plentiful, I had a friend who fished for them often. He had very definite ideas about what good striper fishing was all about. He liked to fish for them only at night, and to surf-cast for them. To his mind, wading into breaking waves and casting a plug into feeding fish by moonlight was the ultimate angling experience.

I joined him occasionally, and, once I had experienced it, I understood his taste for night-time striper fishing.

The largest striper I ever hooked was on a cool, foggy summer night on a beach not far from the Golden Gate. The two of us were waist-deep in the surf—chest-deep when waves rolled in—and we were casting our plugs 50 or 60 yards on surf rods with saltwater spinning reels and 20-pound-test line.

The fish were surely there. Between waves we could hear them as they fed on the surface, and we could see them when the fog lifted off the water from time to time. We were catching plenty—good fish, 6- and 8-pounders, with a few of over 10 pounds.

After each of us had already landed several fish, the feeding intensity increased and the fish moved closer to shore. Stripers were boiling on the surface and slapping the water with their tails. We cast out into the middle of this action, and before our plugs had been drawn more than a few feet across the surface, both of us were into fish.

I knew at once that the fish I'd hooked was at least twice as large as any I had landed until then. Yet, for some reason, I remained calm. It was one of those rare and perfect moments that all fishermen are lucky enough to experience from time to time. I didn't really need to worry about landing this fish, because I knew I would hook several more before we were through.

I stood there in the cool water, comfortable in my chest waders, feeling waves surge by me, listening to them break and roll up the coarse-grained sand beach behind me and then hiss back out again.

The fish fought with powerful surges, and, as I played it, I could hear other striped bass feeding. I smelled the sea, even the fish themselves, as I pumped the rod and worked the fish steadily in. Foghorns were sounding from over on the bay, and sirens far away, as there always seem to be at night in San Francisco.

I could easily have backed up onto the beach and landed my fish that way, on 10 or 15 yards of line. But I felt too happy, too good to move, so I stayed where I was, and because of this I lost the fish. The plug pulled free when he was a few yards away and beginning another strong surge toward deeper water.

I laughed aloud when the hook pulled out, and I felt so good about it all that I stood there for several minutes before I made another cast. I watched my friend land a fish and release it, and I thought about what an excellent pastime fishing is.

I hope striped bass survive, so that anglers a hundred years from now will have a chance to feel what I felt then.

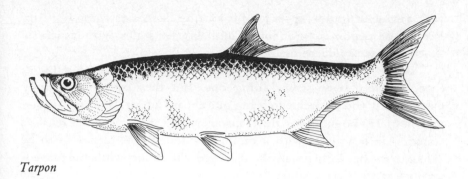

Tarpon

Tarpon

Sometimes tarpon are found in fresh water, sometimes in salt water, but they are ordinarily considered saltwater fish. They are caught in good numbers in Mexico, Nicaragua, Costa Rica, and Panama. Though they can be found in coastal waters on both sides of the Atlantic, they are most numerous and susceptible to anglers along the Florida Keys. Their nearest relative is the herring, and tarpon, which reach weights in excess of 300 pounds, are indeed built and colored like herring, with powerful, compact bodies and large silver scales.

Tarpon are caught by still-fishing, drifting with live or dead bait, or trolling various natural baits as well as spoons, plugs, and lures. However, it is fly-fishing that attracts the most serious anglers to this fish. Landing a large tarpon on a fly rod is thought by some to be the ultimate accomplishment in ocean fishing.

Because a tarpon is a very powerful fish with a tough, bony mouth, using heavy fly tackle is essential. You need a stiff rod to set the hook, and to handle a fish that might run for miles; it's not unusual for a large tarpon to fight for ten or twelve *hours*.

White, yellow, and red are almost always effective fly colors, in either feathers or bucktail. The size of the hook you use depends on the size of the fish expected. A Number 2 hook is adequate for catching tarpon under 20 pounds, and will hook fish of any size, but a 3/0 hook with a wing at least 4 inches long is a better bet for catching big fish. Because of tarpons, tough mouths and abrasive scales, wire leaders or shock tippets should be used.

Like so many premier ocean game fish, tarpon have no value as food, so there is no sense killing one. But they can be extremely dangerous if you do decide to bring one aboard a boat. Hauling a green tarpon of 150 pounds over the transom would make as much sense as stepping into a closet with a mountain lion. If the tarpon is to be released, the hook can usually be removed with pliers while the played-out fish is still in the water.

The good news about fly-fishing for tarpon in the Florida Keys is that the fish are still there in good numbers. The bad news is that because of the encroachment of civilization, it is growing harder and harder to catch them.

Tarpon spend most of their time in deep water, but, for reasons that remain unexplained, they occasionally move onto fairly shallow flats, in the manner of bonefish. They are usually nervous and spookable in shallow water, but this is the place where fly fishermen have a chance at catching them.

For every ten large tarpon hooked, it is doubtful that more than one is landed. They jump wildly at the strike, and usually several times afterwards, and if the hook is not deeply set it is sure to be thrown. If given enough time, their jaws and sides will wear through virtually any line, and if you have a careless moment three or four hours into a fight, they can snap even a sound line.

Tarpon fishing could be described as a shallow-water form of bill-fishing, because it too involves long, hard fights which can thoroughly exhaust an angler. In tarpon fishing there is an alternative, however. Some fishermen prefer to try for tarpon in the 10-to-20-pound range. Fish of this size are magnificent sport on fly tackle, and, with luck, one might hook ten or a dozen of them on a good day. If you hook a large tarpon in the morning, and it stays hooked, chances are your day is complete.

More bad news: Some experienced tarpon fishermen are convinced that fishing in the flats will soon be a thing of the past. There are now too many speedboats and skiers in the water, too many tourists in rubber rafts, and, of course, too many fishermen. The Florida Keys have changed considerably in the last twenty-five years. Tarpon, always nervous, have begun to stay in deeper water. No doubt they will always be catchable out there, but it will be a sad loss if they are permanently frightened away from the shallows. If that happens, the very essence of the sport will disappear.

I consider myself very lucky to have seen the Florida Keys when the fishing there was uncrowded. The first time I ever saw a school of tarpon—fish of 40 pounds or more—was on a calm, cloudy morning in the 1950s. I was camping on Marathon Key, where in those days civilization consisted of little more than a café and a gas station. The only fishing gear I owned was a fairly light bait-casting outfit and a spear, sling, and diving mask.

I'd finished a breakfast of dry bread and oranges and was rowing along in an old wooden skiff, looking for a place to do some spearing. Suddenly, something rolled beside me, so close that it actually rocked the boat. When I stood up to look I saw that I was in the middle of a group of slowly-cruising tarpon—more of them than I could count. I was in no more than 6 feet of water over a sandy bottom, and there they were, swimming lazily on all sides, with no apparent concern about my presence.

I grabbed the rod and made a cast, ahead of the boat and at an angle to the left, toward five fish swimming close together in the same direction. The silver spoon landed about 25 yards away, and as soon as I began to retrieve, one of the five tarpon swerved to follow. It hit before I had the spoon halfway back. I set the hook, but not hard enough, and he threw the spoon on the first wild jump. I heard that fish crash down, like a boulder hitting the water, and watched my silver spoon where he had thrown it high against the gray sky.

I cast again and hooked another fish. This time I set the hook solidly, hitting the tarpon four or five times. He snapped the line—15-pound-test, I believe—on his first furious run.

I had at least ten of the spoons with me that morning, and I lost them all in less than half an hour. If I'd had a hundred spoons along I know I'd never have landed one of those fish. They were immensely powerful, frighteningly so, and I suppose their leaps and runs seemed particularly strong on such a quiet morning. Also, I was out there in a small boat, all alone.

There were good-sized tarpon in that same area nearly every day for a month, and even though I couldn't afford it, I bought adequate tackle and learned how to fish for them. I saw perhaps fifteen other anglers in eight or ten other boats during the entire time. My only regret is that I didn't fish with flies in those days.

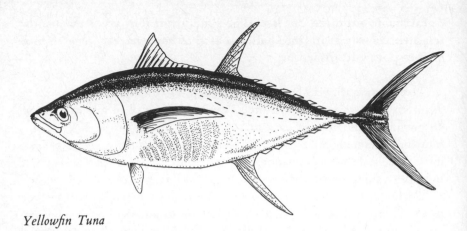

Yellowfin Tuna

Yellowfin Tuna

Though their migratory patterns are unpredictable, yellowfin tuna are found in warm waters around the world. They certainly qualify as moderately large fish. Two-hundred-pounders are caught in Hawaii, and a few individual fish probably grow to weigh more than 300 pounds, but in most areas, the average fish will weigh closer to 30 or 40 pounds.

It could be said that the yellowfin is to the bluefin tuna what the sailfish is to the blue marlin. Fishermen interested in long, grueling fights, and macho status in dockside bars, are likely to fish for bluefins. As with marlin, they may have to wait days or even weeks between fish. Anglers who are willing to settle for fun will be happy with yellowfins.

Yellowfins travel in schools, often huge, always staying in deep water, where they feed on schools of smaller fishes and squid. Often they can be found with porpoises, and most fishermen will troll by a school of rolling porpoises on the chance that tuna are traveling with them. When a school of tuna is located, whether or not it is visibly feeding, fish are usually easy to catch. Trolled feather jigs are the standard lure, and if they don't happen to work, sub-surface plugs sometimes will. Whole dead baits or strip baits can be effective lures,

110

and it is also possible to hook yellowfins on flies—but it isn't always easy to land them. These torpedo-shaped fish are very strong—even stronger than the average ocean game fish—and they are always hooked in deep water. They waste no energy jumping, and their first runs are always down, often all the way to the water's bottom. It takes a rod with backbone to work any tuna of 25 pounds or more back to the surface.

In July of 1983 I took a ten-day fishing trip to Baja, and when I arrived at Loreto I discovered that there were large schools of yellowfin tuna in the area for the first time in several years. Luis, a Mexican fisherman, told me he had caught as many as fifty fish in a single day.

I never came close to fifty a day on that trip, but I did see more tuna than I'd ever seen before or have since. I fished for them three times, motoring out of Nopolo across the glass-smooth sea at daybreak, and always running into a school before the sun rose above Carmen Island. Sometimes there was an area 50 yards across that was alive with feeding fish, causing the surface to roll as thousands of them plowed back and forth through baitfish schools.

They were hitting anything that I dragged by the edge of the commotion. I hooked fish on feathers, plastic squids, plugs, and finally on steelhead flies. The fish ranged in size from 10 to 20 pounds, and as I admired them in the sunlight I realized that they are by far the loveliest of tunas, with pale golden stripes across their backs, bright golden fins, and black dots on their smooth silver bellies.

I was surprised at how powerfully they fought, particularly when I played them on the fly rod. Then, the day I left, I heard a story that convinced me I was lucky I hadn't hooked a really large yellowfin.

A week before I arrived, a fly fisherman had come down from California determined to prove that he could handle yellowfins of any size on fly gear. He used a very stiff fiberglass rod, a saltwater reel with a strong drag, and a 40-pound-test leader. He landed several fish, the largest of them at nearly 50 pounds, but then he hooked one that everyone on the boat figured had to be at least twice that size. The fisherman tightened the drag to stop the tuna's first run, but he didn't stop it. The tuna was so strong that it snapped the rod, stripped the guides from top to bottom, and then pulled the reel out of its seat and into the water. The last anyone saw of the reel, it was a couple of feet beneath the surface and moving out to sea as it sank. I can't be certain this story is true, but based on what I know of yellowfin tuna I'm inclined to believe it.

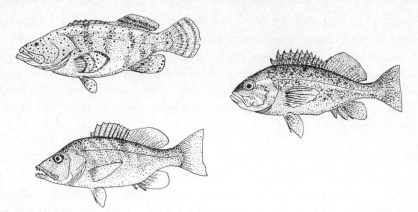

Bottom Fish; Jewfish upper left, *Dog Snapper* lower left, *Vermilion Rockfish* right

A Few Words About Bottomfishing

The shape and color of a fish are usually clear indicators of where and how it lives. Most ocean game fish that are caught by surface trolling are streamlined, with dark backs and white or silver sides and bellies. These fish spend considerable time near the surface as they travel in search of food. Dark-colored fish with broader, more compact bodies usually live at or near the ocean bottoms. Though some of these bottom-dwellers may migrate considerable distances, most of them spend extended periods of time in limited areas. Groupers, snappers, and rockfish, among others, make up this huge group of bottomfish.

There are more than 400 species of groupers alone, found in oceans virtually everywhere. The largest is the jewfish, which can weigh more than 500 pounds. All groupers are predatory, and nearly all are considered good-to-excellent table fish.

Snappers also grow to large sizes—the dog snapper, for example, tops 100 pounds—and they are also fine table fish. Red snapper is the best-known species, but such fish as mangrove snappers and mutton snappers are caught by thousands of anglers.

Rockfish make up another very large family, with about 250 members. In the Pacific many of these species are mistakenly called "rock-cod." Whatever they are called, they too are white-fleshed and delicious. They generally have large heads and mouths, spotted or mottled bodies, and spiny dorsal fins.

Some fishermen spend their lives going after bottomfish, and these fish are a staple of charter boat captains when other species are out of season or proving difficult to catch. At fishing docks nearly everywhere, it is common to see ten or fifteen fishermen filing off a boat at the end of a day carrying burlap sacks loaded down with bottomfish.

Usually these fish are taken on bait. Wherever there is a reef, a rocky bottom, or a wreck, there are bottomfish, and, if located, they are usually fairly easy to catch. Few would argue that they are great sport, however. They are certainly strong, but they don't jump and run the way surface feeders do. Once hooked, a bottomfish will almost always try to return to its ledge or crevice in the rocks. For this reason —and especially if the fish are of any great size—an angler needs a strong rod to keep fish away from trouble. Even a small bottomfish can be impossible to budge once it wedges itself into cover. So, bottomfishing is primarily a tug of war.

In any but the deepest waters, bottomfish can also be caught by trolling or casting. Indeed, they can often be caught on flies. Sometimes, even large groupers and snappers will hit plugs and jigs on the surface just as dorado or tuna will. But when this happens, it still takes a strong rod to handle the fish.

Bottomfishing is done from beaches and piers as well as from boats. Anybody who baits a hook with a fish, a shrimp, a clam, a mussel, or any number of other baits, is almost surely going to catch something. The available species will vary not just from one area to another, but from one beach or bay to another along a small stretch of coastline. Local knowledge is as important here as in other forms of fishing. The same spots usually stay productive year after year.

I've caught my share of bottomfish on plugs and flies, and I also fish for them occasionally with bait. I enjoy cutting the motor off, baiting a hook with a strip of bonito, dropping it to the bottom, and —either drifting or at anchor—sitting on the calm and quiet sea, alone or with a good companion.

113

To hear the birds, the wind, the water itself—these are the reasons I like to bottomfish from time to time. Of course there is also excitement and suspense each time something takes the bait 50, or 100, or 200 feet down. It could be a fish of only 1 pound, or something closer to 100 pounds.

PART THREE

PRACTICAL MATTERS

In discussing practical fishing concerns, my purpose isn't to make specific recommendations about the sizes of rods, types of reels, models of lures, or strengths of lines that should be used in various angling situations. That would be about as pointless as telling somebody which restaurant to go to and exactly what meal to order when there. Anyone who enjoys food makes up his or her own mind about such matters, and any reasonably serious fisherman discovers his or her own preferences through trial and error. My comments are offered in the hope that they will help you eliminate some avoidable errors and make your available choices clearer.

Transition to Salt Water

A freshwater fisherman who decides to try the ocean will be understandably tempted to take his tackle with him, and sometimes this can be a good idea. There are at least two things to keep in mind when making this transition, however. Many anglers who have been fishing for several years own expensive, handmade split-cane rods. These creations are usually worth several hundred dollars apiece, sometimes thousands. To use an old Winston or Powell in the Pacific surf isn't a good idea. Salt water is tough on cane, and so are large fish.

Fiberglass and graphite rods won't be harmed by salt water, but, if they were built for catching trout and bass, they probably won't be of much use in casting the heavy weights and lures often required in ocean fishing, or in handling fish that are larger, faster, and stronger than anything found in rivers or lakes.

When I began to fish with flies in salt water, I was innocent enough to think that my river tackle would be all I ever needed. After all, I had landed steelhead of up to 20 pounds, and chinook salmon considerably larger than that. I soon learned that a 10-pound bonito is about five times as strong as a 20-pound steelhead, and that one dorado running at full speed can burn out a fly reel that has easily handled hundreds of good-sized freshwater fish. I still use my freshwater tackle in the ocean, but only the most resilient, and this is particularly true when it comes to reels.

Whether designed for fresh or salt water, all tackle that is used for ocean fishing should be regularly cleaned. I rinse reels and rods in fresh water at the end of every fishing trip, even if I have been out only an hour or two. Every few weeks I disassemble my reels, scrub them with hot water, grease the working parts, put them back together, and cover all of their surfaces with a film of oil.

Every day, I wash any lures, flies, or hooks I've used with fresh water, and then dry them thoroughly before storing them in their containers.

Boats, too, need care. Fiberglass has come to dominate the small-boat market because it holds up so well in salt water, but even fiberglass needs periodic cleaning and maintenance. Wood needs even more. Motors should be cleaned with fresh water every day, and every few weeks an outboard motor should be run in fresh water to flush out the water pump and slow down the inevitable process of corrosion.

All of these products come with clear care instructions from their manufacturers, and careful attention to these instructions will save every ocean fisherman a great deal of frustration, time, and money.

Tackles

FLY TACKLE

One of the most exciting elements of saltwater fly-fishing is that it is a new sport with unexplored possibilities. As recently as twenty years ago, an angler carrying a fly rod toward the ocean was apt to be greeted with either bewilderment or laughter. These days, hundreds of species of fish are hooked and landed on feathers and bucktail, most surprising considering the size of some of these fish. Sailfish, marlin, and very large tarpon can be handled on 9-foot rods and 12-pound-test leaders.

A point to remember in saltwater fly-fishing is that even very large fish that jump often and spend long periods fighting near the surface *can* be handled using a fly rod and a top-quality reel with a sufficient length of line on it. Using this tackle to catch large fish that sound and hug the bottom is another story. Few people would consider it fun to try to work a large grouper or tuna off the bottom using a long, limber rod.

Even fishermen who don't want to specialize in fly-fishing can make their sport more interesting and enjoyable by taking a fly rod along to the ocean. Whether you are fishing from a boat or from shore, casting opportunities are bound to present themselves. There might be schools of ladyfish, jack cravelle, or bonito feeding on the water's surface. When a dorado is hooked from a boat, it isn't unusual for other dorado to follow it in as the angler plays it, and this presents the fly-caster with a very exciting opportunity. In fact, several ocean species stay with hooked fish and present easy fly-casting targets.

Many fishermen believe that fly-casting is an extremely difficult skill to master, and on lakes and rivers certain kinds of fly-fishing can indeed be difficult. Casting tiny dry flies to feeding trout on smooth, clear water is one of the more challenging tasks in fishing. In the ocean, anybody who can learn to cast out 40 or 50 feet can catch dozens of fish—and anybody willing to practice for half an hour with an experienced caster can learn to do that.

The largest rods and heaviest lines made for salmon and steelhead are fine for fishing in the ocean. Fiberglass or graphite models ranging from 9 to 11 feet and designed to handle numbers 10 to 12 lines are adequate for nearly any ocean-fishing situation. However, many tackle companies, such as Cortland, produce special saltwater fly lines. These lines have tough finishes to withstand hard use, and have extra-heavy forward sections to make long, quick casts easier. Floating lines are desirable for most ocean fishing, because a fly need only be skipped across the surface or sunk an inch or two to draw strikes.

The basic casting technique is simple: If fish are visible, drop the fly near them and then begin to retrieve with hard, rather fast pulls. (An exception here would be with bonefish, which require slower retrieves.) If no targets are visible, cover likely-looking water with repeated casts until you find fish, or until they find you.

Saltwater fly patterns are also simple. Red, white, and yellow are colors used everywhere; blue and green are also widely used. Either feathers or bucktail will work (though bucktail is more durable) and the size of the fly you use is determined by the type of fish you hope to catch. A streamer fly 3 to 4 inches long will catch fish nearly anywhere. Again, anybody who wants to can *learn* to tie a workable saltwater fly in half an hour.

The reel is likely to be the most expensive item in a saltwater fly-fishing outfit. A good, durable, 9-foot rod shouldn't cost much more than $100, but a reel capable of handling ocean fish can easily cost three times that. Even bonefish and bluefish will require 150 yards of 30-pound-test backing behind the fly line (either braided line or monofilament). For larger fish, 300 yards of backing will be necessary.

The drag mechanism on all well-made saltwater reels is smoothly-functioning and dependable, and any tackle salesperson can explain the features which distinguish one model from another. Most fly reels are made with the handle on the right side, which means that if you cast right-handed, you must change hands on the rod once a fish is hooked. All but a few brands of reels can be converted to wind left-hand, however, and many fishermen—especially those used to spinning gear—find this arrangement more comfortable. Most stores will be happy to make the adjustment to left-hand wind when you buy a reel.

Trolling flies isn't as challenging as casting them, but it can be a great deal of fun. It's possible to troll with a fly on a standard fly line and leader, but many anglers rig up a reel without a fly line, so that more monofilament or braided line can be stored on it. The advantage of trolling flies is that even small fish make good sport on a limber and sensitive rod.

121

SPINNING TACKLE

Although the spinning reel was introduced in Europe in 1935, it didn't become popular in America until after World War II. Nowadays, at least nine out of ten beginning fishermen learn to fish with spinning tackle.

The feature that makes a spinning reel easy to use and virtually foolproof is its stationary spool. When a cast is made, the weight of the sinker or lure pulls line from the spool in coils. Because the spool does not have to revolve to free the line there is little resistance, and light sinkers and lures can easily be cast long distances. The stationary spool is therefore fine to use with species such as bonefish. Another advantage of using a spinning reel is that it eliminates the backlashes which can easily occur when using revolving spool bait-casting reels. Finally, the drag on a spinning reel is easily adjustable, and the reel handle remains stationary when a fish takes out line. Because of all these features, anyone of average coordination can learn to handle a spinning reel in a matter of minutes. In fact, some old-timers argue that spinning gear has ruined fishing by making it too easy.

Both braided line and monofilament can be used on spinning reels, though monofilament is by far the most popular material. It is more durable, is less visible to the fish, and allows for longer casts. Braided line is considered better for trolling. With either kind of line, a spinning reel must be filled to within about an eighth of an inch of its capacity before it will operate at full efficiency.

A saltwater spinning reel should be solidly built of corrosion-resistant metals and, above all else, contain a smooth, reliable drag. The spool should hold at least 200 yards of line, even for catching relatively small fish. Closed-face spinning reels—those with the spool enclosed and protected by a metal cover—aren't suited for catching any but the smallest of ocean fish.

Fiberglass and graphite spinning rods run from about 4 to more than 10 feet in length, with actions ranging from soft to very stiff and powerful. The largest spinning rods are made for two-handed casts. Only the larger, stronger models are of much use to saltwater anglers, and the only way to choose a rod is to test its feel and (if possible) cast with it. Any ocean spinning rod should have high-quality guides and a solid, screw-locking reel seat.

Spinning gear is versatile. It can be used to cast from shore or from a boat, for trolling or for bottomfishing. It is also relatively inexpensive. Its major limitation is that the heaviest spinning outfits aren't meant to handle line exceeding 30-pound test. This will do for catching many kinds of ocean fish, but certainly not all.

BAIT-CASTING TACKLE

Bait-casting was the label originally applied to tackle which was developed a century ago to cast live minnows, but today the term applies to any combination of rod and revolving-spool reel.

Bait-casting experts claim two advantages of their gear over spinning tackle. One is that practiced bait-casters can deliver lures, plugs, and baits more accurately and delicately. The other is that a bait-casting outfit simply feels better and is therefore more enjoyable to use.

There is no doubt that, because of the revolving spool, bait-casting is more difficult than spin-casting. If the spool turns too quickly and overruns, a backlash occurs, forming frustrating tangles of line. When a proper cast is made, the spool is controlled by the angler's thumb as the weight of the lure or sinker pulls out line. When the cast is complete and the retrieve begins, the reel gears automatically engage. There is a star-drag system as well. As with spinning, either monofilament or braided line can be used, but monofilament is preferred.

Only the heaviest bait-casting gear is suitable for most ocean fishing. A good-sized rod is needed in order to cast heavy lures and weights, to set the hooks in hard-mouthed fish, and to fight large fish, although anything longer than 6 feet is considered large. Bait-casting tackle will handle approximately the same range of line strengths and line capacities as spinning gear, and can be used for surf-casting, casting from piers or boats, trolling, or bottomfishing.

SURF TACKLE

Any tackle, including fly gear, can be used to catch fish in or near the surf. Nevertheless, a fisherman who wants to specialize in surf-casting will usually use a long, powerful rod which can easily cast heavy weights and lures out more than 100 yards.

An "average" two-handed fiberglass surf rod is about 10 feet long and will handle lures up to a quarter of a pound in weight. Some casters prefer using surf-spinning reels, which are built with extra-wide spools, and some like revolving spool reels, which are often loaded with braided line. This rod is likely to be surprisingly stiff, because "feel" has been sacrificed for the power needed to make long casts.

The best way to decide what kind of surf-casting tackle you will want or need in a given area is to consult tackle shops and local fishermen. They will be familiar with the most useful rods and reels for local fishing conditions, including roughness of water, wind, average casting distance, weights of useful lures, and the size of fish to be expected.

BOAT TACKLE

Boat tackle is meant to be used for trolling or still-fishing, and is necessary to catch the largest ocean fish, including large marlin and tuna. Boat tackle rods are short, stiff, and very powerful. The most expensive of them have roller guides and tips to eliminate wear and reduce friction when big fish make long, fast runs. Rod butts are designed for use with a fighting chair or belt. Reels have revolving spools and easily-adjustable star drags, and large models can hold more than 1000 yards of line that tests at more than 100 pounds. The problem with such heavy boat gear is that when moderate-sized fish such as sailfish and dorado are hooked on it, they have no chance to perform. When trolling for any but the largest game fish, *light* boat gear or bait-casting, spinning, or fly gear will be a distinctly better choice.

Lures

Hundreds and perhaps thousands of lures are available to ocean fishermen. A display in any sporting goods store near an ocean is likely to include a bewildering assortment of models in all shapes, sizes, and colors.

Lure selection is seldom as complicated as such displays would indicate. The basic lures to use in salt water are jigs and plugs. A jig is simply a lead head with feathers attached. Jigs of various sizes and weights fished at various depths will catch fish anywhere. Common jig colors are red, white, yellow, blue, and green in various shades and combinations.

What surprises me is how few ocean fishermen make their own lures. I make a jig that has worked everywhere I've ever used it, a variation of the homemade squid-fly mentioned in "Fishing From a Small Boat." I begin by clamping a 1/4-inch round lead weight to monofilament line. Then with a large needle I poke a hole through the head of the vinyl squid and slide the squid down the line until its head is snugly fitted over the lead weight. Next, I tie a treble hook to the lower end of the monofilament line so that it is hidden by the vinyl strips that form the body of the squid. The entire operation takes no more than a minute or two, and for less than 50¢ I have a lure that would cost at least $3.00 in any sporting goods or tackle store. I make these jigs in different colors and trim them to various sizes, and they can be cast or trolled. I also make casting and trolling lures out of feathers and bucktail, which are even cheaper than squids.

Plugs are most often made of wood or plastic and are meant to represent baitfish. They too can be fished either deep down or on the surface, and are easy to make. Anyone who can shape a piece of wood into something like the body of a fish, paint it, and attach a hook to it can make a good plug.

If you don't choose to make your own lures, you'll generally be better off buying the simple models. Plugs with built-in actions are seldom as effective as those made to be trolled or retrieved without any vibration or darting motion.

Wherever you fish, specific lure types and colors are bound to be favored by local fishermen. These preferences are partly a matter of habit. A feeding fish that sees something that looks edible is likely to strike at it. I have no doubt that an ocean fisherman could do fairly well trolling cigars, bananas or alka-seltzer bottles. The notion that lures are designed to appeal to fishermen rather than fish is especially true in regard to saltwater angling.

Baits

Natural baits used in salt water include crabs, clams, mussels, sand worms, squids, and eels. Many species of small- to moderate-sized fishes are used as bait. Among the most common of these are sardines, mackerel, herring, anchovies, and halfbeaks. For catching big game fish, baits such as bonito and flying fish of up to 10 pounds are standard. Baits are fished alive or dead, whole or in strips or chunks. They can be fished on the bottom, or held near the surface with floats. They can be trolled, cast, and retrieved, or allowed to drift or swim naturally on an unweighted hook.

Many anglers buy their baits on piers or in dockside tackle shops. Such sources aren't always reliable, however, and they charge rather high prices.

It's often possible, and sometimes fairly easy, to collect or catch your own bait. Clams can be gathered at low tide on many beaches, and mussels can easily be taken from the wooden pilings on piers.

Baitfish are bound to be abundant in any productive fishing area, because it is the baitfish that *make* the area productive. They can often be taken on small jigs or with tiny hunks of baits such as mussel or clam. When baitfish

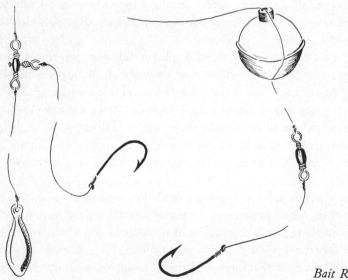

Bait Rigs

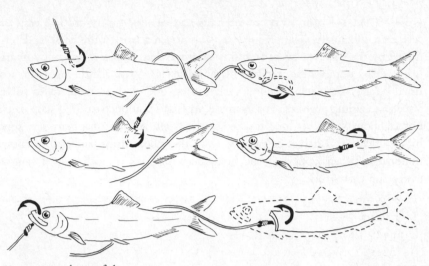

How to Hook Baitfish

school up in clear water near shore, they can be captured in a cast net, or snagged.

When good numbers of baitfish are swimming near the surface, it is usually possible to snag them in blue water a mile or more offshore. The best thing about snagging, wherever you are, is that you will probably be fishing with the same bait that game fish are actively feeding on.

Once, on a Mexican pier, I watched an expert snagger keep half a dozen of his friends supplied with bait throughout an afternoon. Large schools of halfbeaks (or balao) were cruising back and forth in front of the pier, a few feet beneath the surface of the calm, clear water. Every few minutes a school of sierra or a pair of dorado ripped through the halfbacks, scattering them wildly.

Using a spinning rod and casting an ounce of lead with four treble hooks tied at 6-inch intervals above it, the snagger cast into the halfbeaks as soon as they had reassembled after a sierra or dorado attack. Then he retrieved in long, fast, powerful pulls, and snagged at least one halfbeak on every cast. His friends were using handlines and hooking the halfbeaks under their dorsal fins, then tossing them into the water to swim freely. The sierras and dorados quickly attacked the hooked halfbeaks, and before the afternoon was over the handliners had caught several dozen of them.

Even the most dedicated fly or lure fisherman will admit that sometimes bait works better than anything else, and sometimes it is the *only* thing that

127

works. There are many ways to rig baits so that they can be trolled, cast, or retrieved effectively. The precise way you attach a bait to the hook is determined by the way you want to fish it, and by what species of baitfish you are using. Diagrammed here are some of the basic rigs. With a little ingenuity it's usually fairly simple to devise a variation on one of these methods to solve a specific angling problem. For example, in Baja I was once trolling strip baits, bonito about six inches long hooked at the front. As often happens, fish kept biting off the rear halves or ripping away the whole strips, and still escaping unhooked. When I put a second hook near the back of each strip, I caught every fish that struck.

Lines

Nowadays, most fishermen use monofilament lines, which have been improved greatly in recent years. Monofilament manufactured by any of the well-known tackle companies will be of high and dependable quality. The major consideration when choosing line is the pound-test rating, which is based on a number of factors: size of fish expected, weight of sinker or lure to be cast or trolled, strength of rod, and reel capacity. Ocean fish are seldom leader-shy, so, unless you are hoping for a record fish on a particular-strength line, it usually makes sense to use the strongest line that a rod and reel can practically handle. If you are fishing with a fly or spinning rod, landing a 10-pound jack cravelle on 20-pound-test line is just as much fun as landing it on 6-pound test. The advantage of the heavier line is that you don't have to check it for wear so often. Also, if you plan to release the fish you catch, you can get it back in the water more quickly and let it go in better condition.

Even though most ocean fish don't seem to be bothered by the sight of heavy lines, it makes sense to match monofilament to the color of the water you are fishing, making your line virtually invisible. Oceans are usually either blue, green, or brownish, and line comes in these shades.

Many experts recommend braided Dacron™ or nylon for trolling, because it doesn't have as much stretch as monofilament. Sending 60 or 80 yards of line out behind your boat makes it easier to set hooks. Braided lines are more visible than monofilament, so many anglers who troll with nylon or Dacron™ attach a monofilament leader to it with a swivel. Another disadvantage of braided lines is that they aren't as durable as monofilament (though perhaps they soon will be, as manufacturers steadily improve their products). No matter what kind of line you use, you should cut off a few feet up front after landing a large fish, or at the end of each fishing day.

Line of any kind comes in spools that hold anywhere from 25 to more than 1000 yards of it. It's a very good idea to buy a spool large enough to fill a reel without your having to splice pieces of line together. Knots weaken with age, and many good fish have been lost because lines snapped at old splices.

When filling a reel, be sure to wind new line on evenly, and with a fairly heavy tension. After playing a fish, make sure that line has also been recovered evenly. This is especially necessary to do with all fly reels and some bait-casting and trolling reels. If the line isn't spooled evenly, strip it off and rewind it.

Even when using the best swivels, line gets twisted, from both trolling and playing fish. The best way to straighten twisted line is to cut off the lure or hook and drag the twisted portion freely behind the boat. This is especially effective at high speed, perhaps on the way in at the end of a day. After a few minutes of dragging the line will be as straight as new.

Replace old line every couple of seasons, or more often if you fish regularly. Sun and salt water combined with heavy use will weaken any line, no matter how well you care for it.

Knots

For every fish that is lost because of worn or weak line, at least twenty are lost because of faulty knots. Probably the most common mistake that fishermen make when they tie knots is not pulling them tight enough. Pull any knot you tie as tightly as you can to test it. If necessary, use gloves so that the line won't cut your hands. If a knot can't take all the pressure you can apply, it won't stand up to a good fish, either.

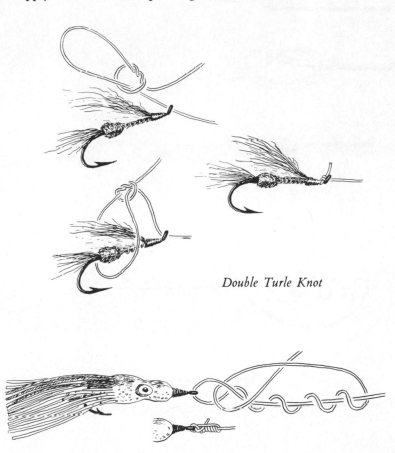

Double Turle Knot

Improved Clinch Knot

The knots that attach hooks, lures, and swivels should be retied after catching each good fish, or after every few hours spent fishing. Not many anglers are willing to take the time to do this, but there are many who end up wishing they had when "the fish of the year" (or of a lifetime) is hooked near the end of a day and breaks off at a weakened knot.

Diagrammed here are the basic knots that every fisherman needs.

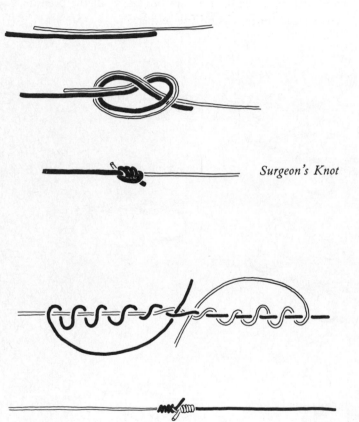

Surgeon's Knot

Blood Knot

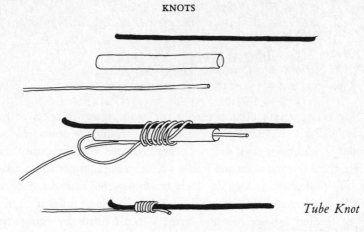

Tube Knot

Reading Water

Nowadays, it isn't often necessary to "read" water in order to find fish. In any well-known fishing area, the most productive spots are common knowledge. On most days, such spots are crowded with fishermen. Happily, though, there are still times and places where an ocean fisherman can be alone, with only ingenuity as a guide. Then reading water becomes important.

Whether you are casting from shore or trolling lures miles at sea, the surest signs of feeding fish are bait and birds. When baitfish are being chased by predators, one, two, or even a dozen often leap from the water in panic. Most likely, the fish that are chasing the bait will show too, slicing through the water, sometimes jumping as they close in on their prey. There are few sights in fishing as exciting as a school of feeding yellowfin tuna, striped bass, or jack cravelle. On calm days their activity can be seen from hundreds of yards away.

When baitfish have been driven to the surface, birds soon arrive on the scene. Pelicans, frigatebirds, and gulls by the score will circle and dive over a mass of baitfish and can be spotted from many miles away.

When there are no fish or birds visible in an area, there may still be good fishing there. If the water is clear it is easy enough to spot underwater rocks, ledges, holes, and drop-offs from shore or from a high point on the beach such as a rock or tree, especially if the tide is low. From a good vantage point it is usually possible to pick out currents and riptides, which are gathering places for fish. Turbulent water is a better indicator than still water.

Casting from shore in Baja, there is a sure and simple way to locate fish: near rocky cliffs on sandy beaches. Sometimes, this will mean a cliff only 20 yards long and half as high, with half a mile or more of sand on either side of it. Over the years, chunks of rock have dropped from these cliffs into the water, and the rocks provide the only good cover for fish in the area. Baitfish have gathered there, as well as cabrilla, dog snappers, jack cravelle, roosterfish, and ladyfish. Some or all of them are there for the baitfish, depending on the time of day or year.

At night, surf-casters sometimes rely on sound and smell rather than on sight to find fish. When fish are feeding wildly near shore, which is fairly common after dark, they can be heard even above the roar and hiss of breaking waves. Also, striped bass and bluefish are said to give off a smell like fresh cucumbers or melons.

Many highly-prized game fish have habits that sometimes make them easy to find. Schools of tuna very often travel with porpoises, and when porpoises are rolling on the surface they are visible from great distances. Dorado like to rest under anything that floats on the surface, and sometimes several fish are caught from underneath an old wooden box or a driftwood log. A friend of mine once stopped his boat 20 yards from a patch of floating seaweed in deep blue water on the Sea of Cortez. Casting a surface plug toward the weed, he caught twenty-one large dorado from underneath it. Several years ago near La Paz, it is said that a victim of a drowning was spotted by fishermen. When they got close enough, they saw dorado holding beneath the floating corpse. They caught the fish before they recovered the body.

At moderate depths in clear water, when the bottom can be seen, it is always worth fishing over and around large rocks and ledges, or channels of sand between rocky areas. Offshore islands are a likely place to find these conditions. In deep water, any visible current, upwelling, or unusual movement of water is worth trolling by or casting toward at least once.

When you catch a good fish because you have seen signs and interpreted them correctly, the feeling of accomplishment that comes with any successful fishing is intensified.

Safety

Each year, the oceans kill hundreds of fishermen. Sometimes, this is because surf-casters wade in farther than they should and are carried off and drowned by strong tides and currents. Sometimes they walk off the edge of a ledge or sandbar and are dragged down by the weight of heavy clothing. Sometimes they are hit by wave-tossed logs.

In Hawaii, I once walked and climbed along a series of rocks and tide pools against the face of a steep cliff, looking for a place to fish for *ulua*. Half a mile from the beach I'd started from I found my spot, but before I caught anything I noticed that the tide was rising. I started back, but before I was halfway to the safety of the sand beach, the tide pools and rocks were submerged, and finally I had to swim back. I saved my rod, but lost my tackle box. If I'd gone much farther along the rocks, or if large waves had come up—as they often do in that area—I could have lost my life. I was never so stupid again.

Each year, hundreds of lives are also lost in boats. Such deaths occur because fishermen in small boats go too far out, or go out without checking weather forecasts, or speed through unfamiliar waters and hit reefs or barely submerged rocks, or pass too close to shore and are overturned or swamped by waves, or fail to maintain their motors properly, and find themselves suddenly adrift without power when a storm comes up.

The 1985 California ocean-salmon season opened on Saturday, February 16. Dozens of boats went out to fish near the mouth of the Salinas River in the Monterey area. It was a foggy day with large swells rolling in, but good fishing was predicted, and people went anyway. Ten of them drowned when their boats were overturned.

No list of guidelines can cover every precaution that should be taken at sea, or every possible emergency that might arise, but common sense and respect for nature are basic. A calm sea is a very deceptive place, because at any time of year in any climate, it can change very suddenly.

There are precautions, however, that every ocean fisherman should take. It always makes sense to fish with a partner, so that help is there if anything does go wrong. Any boat of any size should be equipped with life jackets, food and water, a flashlight or flares, a bailing can or pump, and oars or paddles (if not an auxiliary motor). Having a radio on board has saved much inconvenience and many lives each year. When fishing an unfamiliar area, either from shore or from a boat, extreme care should always be exercised. If navigational charts and maps are available, use them.

I went on a spear-fishing trip when I was sixteen years old. A friend and I had anchored our outrigger canoe about a mile off Waikiki, and we were diving over a reef about 50 yards from the boat. It was a clear, calm day, but, after two or three hours out there, I noticed a wall of black clouds moving toward us form over the mountain valleys. By the time we reached the canoe, it was raining hard. Before we had paddled halfway in, wind was howling and rain was pounding down in torrents. The rain was so loud that we couldn't hear each other, even when we screamed. We could barely see each other at opposite ends of the canoe. We were healthy boys in good physical condition, but it took us more than two hours to make it to shore. We were nearly swamped several times, and by the time we did reach the beach we were exhausted.

In another incident, on a November morning in Baja, Hilde and I were heading out in our inflatable, the *Zucarita*. As soon as we left Escondido Bay we realized that we shouldn't go far, because there were already large swells rolling in from the northeast, and the wind was gusting from the same direction. So we trolled flies just outside the bay, hoping for sierra or dorado. About an hour after we'd started, a large cabin cruiser with three young men aboard sped by us, heading for the offshore islands several miles away.

I figured they might be heading for trouble, and I was right. By 10:00 that morning the weather was awful, with strong winds making the sea very choppy and waves breaking everywhere. Hilde and I headed in at once.

The weather worsened, and the three young men didn't get back for thirty-six hours. Their main motor went out just as they turned to head back, when they were about 5 miles out at sea. They had a 7-horsepower auxiliary outboard, but minutes after they had it started, it was swamped and ruined, permanently, by breaking waves. The wind blew them farther to sea, and luckily they finally hit an island. There they stayed through the night, cold and miserable, on a rocky beach without protection from the storm. They stayed there through most of the next day too, after the weather had calmed. Finally, a Mexican fisherman came by and towed them back to Escondido.

They were among the lucky ones.

Playing Fish

Successfully bringing a fish to a boat or shore is a matter of luck, instinct, knowing the limits of your tackle, and knowing how to use it. The process can be divided into three stages: hooking, playing, and landing the fish.

Most saltwater fish strike hard at baits and lures, particularly trolled and retrieved ones, and very often they hook themselves before they make their first frantic runs for freedom. However, many species have tough mouths, so it is always best to set the hook and make sure it is in securely. At the strike, this means raising the rod sharply against the drag of the reel and the weight of the fish. Once a fish has completed its first run, three or four sharp jerks in quick succession will assure that the hook is in to stay.

Two mistakes that beginning anglers make while playing fish are cranking the reel handle frantically and continuously (even as a fish is running out line) and tightening the drag when a fish is running. When a fish is running, there is nothing to do but to let it. The farther it gets from the fisherman, the more drag there is from the line in the water, so the drag of the reel should probably be *loosened* during the run.

Many species jump wildly at the strike and several times afterwards, especially during the first few minutes of the fight. When this happens, it is customary to lower the rod tip toward the fish, which creates slack line and lessens the chance of a break-off.

When a fish quiets down and its first bursts of energy and panic have been expended, the real fight begins. Now a fisherman must gain control of the situation, tire the fish by applying steady pressure, and regain lost line. Obviously the amount of pressure that can be safely applied depends on the strength of line being used. Most fishermen underestimate their lines; a large fish can easily tow a small boat on 20-pound-test in which all knots have been correctly tied.

When regaining line, you should always pump the rod. Raise the rod smoothly against the strain of the fish, and then quickly lower it again, creating slack line. As you lower the rod, wind quickly to put that slack on the reel.

It usually isn't difficult to tell when a fish is tired enough to be landed. It will stay on or very near the surface, sometimes turning onto its side, unable to dive against the pressure of rod and line. Many fish are still lost at this point, however. Unless the fish is fairly small and the line relatively heavy—for example, an 8-pound dorado or jack on 20-pound-test—it is always a mistake to grab the leader to lift the fish into the boat. If you aren't using a net or gaff, it is possible to grab many ocean fish by the narrow wrists of their tails, provided you are wearing a glove and have a strong grip. Large fish should always be netted or gaffed, or cut free while still in the water. Fish can't swim backwards, so they should be netted head-first: simply slide the net under them and lift. A gaff should be drawn across a fish or up from underneath it, with care taken not to disturb the line. On a beach, the best way to land a fish is to slide it up onto the sand with the rod and several yards of line. On a rocky shore, a gaff or net is again necessary. Of course, all fish of great size, or with bills or sharp teeth, should be handled with extreme caution.

For years now freshwater anglers who care about their sport's future have been releasing most or all of the fish they catch. We now realize that even the oceans are a limited resource, and releasing fish is becoming an important practice in salt water.

Fishing is too fine a sport for us not to want to save it.

Index

Acid rain, effect of on striped bass population, 104
Africa, and bluefish, 74, 75
Aholehole, 17, 18
Alaska, 5
  barracuda, 71
  salmon, 94–95
Amberjacks, 32
Atlantic bluefin tuna, *see* Tuna
Aveveo, 17, 18

Bait-casting tackle, 123
Baits, 126–28
  for barracuda, 71
  for bonefish, 78
  for bonito, 81
  for bottomfish, 113
  for California yellowtail, 84
  chum for bluefish, 75
  for cod, 87
  for king mackerel, 89
  for Pacific salmon, 95
  for sailfish, 96
  for sharks, 99
  for skipjack tuna, 102
  for striped bass, 105
  for tarpon, 107
  for yellowfin tuna, 110
Baja, Mexico, fishing in, 33–34, 134
  barracuda, 71, 72
  bonito, 82–83
  California yellowtail, 84–86
  yellowfin tuna, 111
Barracuda, 70–73, 82
Bierce, Ambrose, 11

Blacktip shark, 99, 100
Blood knot, 132
Bluefish, 32, 74–76, 134
Blue shark, 99
Boats:
  bluefish, fishing for from, 75
  care of, 118
  cod, fishing for from, 87–88
  equipment for, 136
  fishing from a large, 57–66
  fishing from a small, 39–55
  inflatable, 39
  king mackerel, fishing for from, 89–90
  striped bass, fishing for, 105
  tackle for, 124
Bonefish, 27, 77–80
Bonito, 7, 9, 43, 50, 61, 71, 81–83, 102, 118
Bonito sharks, 99
Bottomfishing, 112–14
Brazil, and barracuda, 70

Cabrilla, 47, 50
California:
  and barracuda, 71
  and bonito, 81
  and salmon, 95
  and striped bass, 104–105
California yellowtail, 84–86
Canada, and striped bass, 105
Cane rods, and salt water, 118
Cannon, Ray, 52
Carolinas, and cod, 87
Casting:
  for barracuda, 71
  for bluefish, 75

141